MW01282343

I am *Not* an ISLAND

Discovering My True Foundation

Shelby Drinnon

WESTBOW
P R E S S®
A DIVISION OF THOMAS NELSON
& ZONDERVAN

WestBow Press books may be ordered through booksellers or by contacting:

WestBow Press
A Division of Thomas Nelson & Zondervan
1663 Liberty Drive
Bloomington, IN 47403
www.westbowpress.com
1 (866) 928-1240

Scripture quotations are taken from the Holy Bible, New Living Translation, copyright ©1996, 2004, 2015 by Tyndale House Foundation. Used by permission of Tyndale House Publishers, a Division of Tyndale House Ministries, Carol Stream, Illinois 60188. All rights reserved.

ISBN: 978-1-9736-9525-7 (sc)
ISBN: 978-1-9736-9526-4 (e)

Library of Congress Control Number: 2020911763

Print information available on the last page.

WestBow Press rev. date: 6/30/2020

To my wonderful husband, who travels this life with me. Thank you for your support and love. To my parents and siblings, who were always there for me, I love you.

"I want you all to know about the miraculous signs and wonders the Most High God has performed for me." Daniel 4:2. This is not my story. This is God's story of love and redemption that He is telling through my family. God is the giver of all good things, and God gave me the idea for this book. I remember hearing in my heart, plain as day, "I am going to write a book." I didn't know how, and I didn't know when. I told Stetson that I was going to write a book about our story, and he said, "Giddy up." So, here it is. I am not a writer, nor did I ever aspire to be one. God had a plan for my life though, and He told me to tell my side of this story through this book, so I am being obedient. Stetson tells his side of the story verbally and shares it with anyone who will listen. I am telling my side of the story through a book. (Is anyone surprised the different ways we both chose to share?) I sat down at the computer one day and the words flowed from me. God was pouring our story out through me so that our testimony could help others overcome. "And they have defeated him by the blood of the Lamb and by their testimony." Revelations 12:11. Our testimony is the story of God's grace, mercy, and love. I pray that through this story you will find God's grace, mercy, and love for yourself.

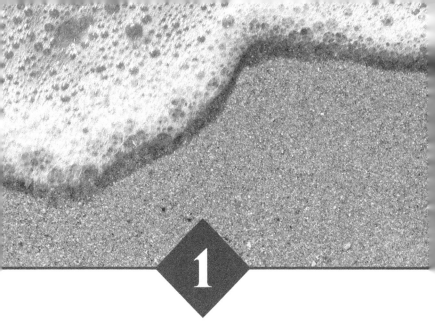

The Beginning

"In the beginning God created the heavens and the earth. The earth was formless and empty, and darkness covered the deep waters. And the Spirit of God was hovering over the surface of the waters."

Genesis 1:1-2

B eginnings are not easy, smooth, or graceful. Beginnings can be messy, ugly, and full of disorder. Much like the beginning of a relationship. Getting to know a new person and navigating the terrain of dating a hopeful girlfriend or boyfriend is neither smooth nor graceful. Personally, it's awkward. When I think about the beginning of my relationship with my husband, smooth and graceful is not what comes to mind. Ugly, ridiculously messy, and packed with disorder is how I would describe it.

This could also describe the beginning of my relationship with my Lord and Savior. As the earth was formless and empty before creation, so was I formless and so very empty. "Darkness covered the deep waters." In the beginning, I was an island, surrounded by darkness and deep waters, threatening to engulf me. But just like the beginning of this world, the Spirit of God was hovering. Dear friend, I pray that as you read through this book about the struggles, trials, and temptations I encountered, and the wonderful grace of our Lord that I discovered through the hard times, it will encourage you and strengthen you.

◆ ◆ ◆

I grew up in a very small town, population around 500. Since this was smack dab in the middle of the Bible Belt, almost everybody I knew went to church, as well as my family. Growing up in church, attending church camp every summer, and having a loving mother who told me about God led me to accept the Lord into my heart at an early age. As far back as I can remember, my mother would wake me up early to have a bible lesson. I would sleepily walk into the living room, lay my head on her lap, and listen to the Word of God as she read. I was hearing the loving words of my Lord before I could even understand them. My mom was speaking life words over me and praying God's love and goodness for me. My dad only went to church with us on Christmas and Easter. I never really questioned it or wondered why. That was just the way it was. When I was

8, I was baptized. I remember watching the older kids get baptized and I knew that is what I wanted for my life. I did not fully understand why I did, but I had a yearning in my heart to show my love for God. I was always involved in our church's youth group as I grew. We would attend Christian concerts, Sunday night church, and multiple church camps every summer. As I entered high school, I continued to go to all these Christian events. However, I never fell deeply in love with God. I never had a deep, fiery passion to draw closer to Him. I would describe my relationship with the Lord as on the fence. On Sundays, I would go to church, listen to the preacher (sometimes), and go home. On Sunday nights, I would go to youth group with my friends, and then do whatever my sinful heart desired. The rest of the week, I would live my life the way I wanted to, not considering the Lord and his desires for my life. I loved God, but I did not fully understand His love for me. I did not understand how He loved me, so I did not know how to love Him the way that I should have. I was lukewarm in my love for God. In Revelations 3:15-16 God says, "'I know all the things you do, that you are neither hot nor cold. I wish that you were one or the other! But since you are like lukewarm water, neither hot nor cold, I will spit you out of my mouth!'" My life was not pleasing God. I was lukewarm water and God desired me to be hot. But to make water hot, it must be put to the fire. I was a lukewarm Christian that needed fire from the Holy Spirit. God intended to give me that fire, but I had to first go through the fire. I had to first endure trials to purify me and make me the hot water that was desirable to God. 1 Peter 1:6-7 says, "So be truly glad. There is wonderful joy ahead, even though you must endure many trials for a little while. These trials will show that your faith is genuine. It is being tested as fire tests and purifies gold-though your faith is far more precious than mere gold. So when your faith remains strong through many trials, it will bring you much praise and glory and honor on the day when Jesus Christ is revealed to the whole world." The Lord did not want me to be lukewarm, and he did not want my faith to be false. He wanted me to have a genuine faith in Him. God desired me to be on fire for Him with an all-consuming faith.

Softball was also a very important part of my life in high school. I loved everything about it from the smell of the grass to the feel of dirt under my cleats. I was very confident in my abilities as a player. I loved playing, I loved my team, and I loved having my friends playing with me. My friends were very important to me and I loved to spend time with them. While I also enjoyed being at home and reading a good book, I would never turn down time with my friends. I had a few close friends that I loved like family. Those friends also grew up in church and went to all the Christian things I did. They knew the love of God just like I did. Having friends like that was such a blessing. Then like most girls in high school, I started to take an interest in boys. As I look back on my time in high school with more wisdom and more years lived, I can see that the main reason I took an interest in boys, is that I wanted to feel *chosen*. I wanted to feel like I mattered to someone. So I began hanging out with different people, different boys who would make me feel like I was important. I began drinking as well, not because I liked it but because I thought it made people look at me and think that I was "cool". Goodness, isn't that so cliché? I began doing things like hanging out with boys and drinking because I wanted to feel good and included. I still loved being with my friends, but something was making me feel empty and I needed more to be filled up. Dear friend, I needed God in my life. I felt empty because I did not have the One who created me living inside of me. I had begun stuffing worldly things and worldly feelings inside myself hoping to make myself feel better, to feel *chosen*. I could feel that I wanted more, but I was looking for it in the wrong places. God had already chosen me, but I was not aware of that because I was not looking to Him. I was drifting from the truth of God that my mother had instilled in me.

I began choosing to disobey and lie to my parents. I began lying to them about where I was going or who I was with. There were people that I chose to hang out with that I knew they disapproved of. So instead of listening to them and honoring them, I did what my sinful nature wanted. I knew this was wrong, and I hated disappointing them, but I wanted to feel full and complete. I was filling myself with the wrong kind of pleasure. I chose the wrong path over and over. I had stopped choosing the path my mother was trying to lead me down. I was not waking up early, filling my heart with God's word anymore. I was following the wider path that consisted of fulfilling my flesh. These desires were coming from the whispers of Satan telling me to do what makes me momentarily happy. Satan was lying to me, telling me that partying, drinking, lying, and deceiving was the way to fulfill myself. Satan told me that this was the wat to feel chosen. And I listened. I was moving away from God's love and His truth. While I was trying to fill myself up, I was isolating myself. Worldly things do not last. Everything I was filling myself up with did not stay long because it did not satisfy me. I moved from one drinking buddy to the next trying to find satisfaction, one boy to hang out with to the next, but I never found satisfaction. Until one day, something new happened.

Living in such a small town, everyone knew everyone. You start Pre-school with the same people that you graduate with, so new kids were very exciting. During my junior year, we got a new boy. Imagine Zac Efron with long hair (swoon). It did not take me long to realize that this boy, named Stetson, was special. Or crazy. It was a fine line. He was a ball of energy and radiated smiles. He was one of those people that attracts others and he still is. I started to get to know him, and he was also kind and sweet. He was so much fun to be around. He had an energy for life that was exciting, and he loved to make people laugh. I wanted to be around him because he had this ability to make you feel special. He must have thought I was special too (eventually) because he wanted to spend time with me as well. We began to spend a lot of time together our senior year, until finally one day, he asked me to be his girlfriend.

As we started to date at the end of our senior year, I drifted from God even more, also from my family, and friends. I began to try to fill the isolation and the emptiness that I was feeling up with Stetson. I chose to spend the majority of my time with Stetson. It wasn't a lot at first, but as time went on, I noticed myself wanting to spend all my time with Stetson, with no room for anyone else. I wanted to feel loved and chosen, and he made me feel those things. I thought that he was what I had been searching for. I thought that a boy could be everything that I needed. While Stetson was very kind and sweet, he was not all that I needed. I was not looking towards my future. I was so caught up in the moment that I did not stop to think about what would happen if he was gone. This is just like anything in your life that is not Jesus Christ. I knew about Jesus and loved him, just like I loved God, but I was not *in* love with God. I did not understand that Jesus needed to be my foundation, my cornerstone. It is not enough to just *know* about Jesus. We must invite Him into our lives and allow Him to fill us. He must be what we turn to, and what we rely on. Nothing on earth can fill us and satisfy us like Jesus can. Psalms 107:9 speaks about God saying, "For He satisfies the thirsty and fills the hungry with good things." We are all hungry and desire something, but only God can fill us with *good* things that keep us filled and whole. The things of the world *keep* us hungry and thirsty. We will never be satisfied if we are not seeking to fill ourselves with the Living Water. Jesus speaks in John 4:13-14 saying, "'Anyone who drinks this water will soon become thirsty again. But those who drink the water I give will never be thirsty again. It becomes a fresh, bubbling spring within them, giving them eternal life.'" Without the Living Water that Jesus fills us with, we will be forever empty. I was drinking earthly water, which was only making me thirstier. I could never be filled up and refreshed relying on a human. I was on the path to be forever empty, filling myself with a human's love and not the eternal love of my Heavenly Father.

I continued to choose the path the world and Satan told me to go down. I continued to choose Stetson over friends and family, making him my center, my foundation, and cornerstone. The isolation that lying and drinking had caused now pushed me into a dependent relationship. I was depending on Stetson for fulfillment. When you choose to center your life on a person, instead of our Heavenly Creator, your desires become worldly and life becomes shaky. No matter how special you think the person is, no matter how godly they seem to be, nothing can take the place that Jesus, the true cornerstone, should have in your life. Isaiah 28:16 says "Therefore, this is what the Sovereign Lord says: 'Look! I am placing a foundation stone in Jerusalem, a *firm* and tested stone. It is a precious cornerstone that is safe to build on. Whoever believes need *never be shaken.'*" Jesus Christ is our precious cornerstone, our foundation to build our lives on. Any other cornerstone is bound to break up and crumble because it is not firm. When storms come and life gets hard, Jesus Christ does not waver. God Himself tells us that Jesus is safe to build on because He is firm. Jesus is the one and only foundation that will never be shaken. Matthew 7:24-27 tells us that only a fool would build their house on anything other than rock, the firm and tested stone that is Jesus Christ. I did not believe fully and have my foundation built on the precious cornerstone that is Jesus Christ. I was building my foundation on Stetson. I was being the fool.

I no longer desired to go to church. I was distanced from my parents because I no longer desired their Godly and right company. I could feel the tensions growing between us, and I felt so much guilt for the times that I had lied and deceived them for my own selfish gain. But I loved how I felt chosen when I was with Stetson. I would tell my parents we were just going to the river to swim or sit up town, when in reality, we were drinking, smoking, and driving way too fast. I felt shame and guilt every time I lied, but I just shoved it down hoping the happiness I felt when I was with Stetson would drown it out.

We graduated, and summer flew by like a blur. I had spent

most of the summer with Stetson, making foolish and worldly decisions. Time came for me to go to college and I was not ready. I may have been ready to live away from my parents and have more freedom to see Stetson whenever I wanted, but I was not ready for the rude awakening that came with college.

2

The Descent

1 Peter 5:8: "Your adversary the devil walks about like a roaring lion, seeking whom he may devour."

Stetson and I both went to the same college about two hours away from our hometown. All my other friends were either still in high school or attended other colleges. He signed on to play baseball at this college and I signed on to play softball. I was so excited to play softball and continue the sport that I loved. I did not know what my major would be or what subjects I wanted to study, but I knew that I could play softball. I had no aspirations for my life other than to enjoy college. I did not know what I wanted my future to look like, nor did I care. So I was just momentarily trying to fill myself up each day. My mother and I arrived at my dorm room, which I shared with a stranger. We unpacked and I was immediately flooded with information about what all I needed to do to ensure I was ready for practices, classes, and survival on my own. I realized that college might be a little harder and more nerve-wracking than I was expecting. I was extremely nervous about all the new things that lay ahead of me. I have never felt comfortable with the unknown. In high school, I knew all my classmates and all my teachers. I had known them since I was born. I knew where all my classes were, and I knew what to expect from each class. As soon as my mom left me to go back home, the nervousness compounded. I realized all the comforts of home were gone. I was in a strange place, with strange people, and there were many things about college that I did not know or understand. I went and found Stetson immediately. My dependency on him was growing. I was building my foundation on him more and more. I was unsure of what to do and unsure of where to go, so I turned towards Stetson. I was depending on him for a lot of things, but, if our dependency lies on another human, we will be disappointed. Had my dependency been on my Holy Creator, who created me to depend on Him, I could have avoided the suffering that lay ahead. I could have been sure in what I was meant to do and be confident. Proverbs 3:5-6 says "Trust in the Lord with all your heart; do not depend on your own understanding. Seek his will in all you do, and he will show you which path to take." I was neither depending on the Lord nor seeking His will, therefore, I was unsure of which paths to take. Going off to college, which is a world full of unknowns, caused me to feel vulnerable and insecure. This is where Satan loves to instill fear in people. He whispers insecurities into your mind, making you unsure. Instead of seeking out courage and comfort in the Holy One who created me, I looked to a mere human for these things. Since my dependency lay incorrectly, my paths were not clear. I had no idea what to do or where to go, therefore I made poor choices, created from fear that took me down the wrong path. Satan uses fear to push us away from God, away from what is good and right. He was using fear to push me onto an island of isolation, and I was allowing it to happen.

I spent as much time as possible with Stetson those first few days before classes. Meeting new people is stressful for me so I chose to stick with what was familiar. As the time came for me to start going to softball practices and to class, I felt overwhelmed. I had no clue where my classes were, I had no clue where the softball field was, and I had no clue who these strange people were that I suddenly lived with, who I thought were probably way better at softball than I was. As an introvert who becomes overwhelmed about the thought of asking for extra ketchup at a restaurant, the task of asking a stranger all these mounting questions was daunting. Stetson had started going to baseball practice, so he was not always around. Without him there, I felt lost and alone. I could feel the pressure pushing me into a corner. I could feel my anxiety rising to the surface to overwhelm me. I could feel the fear of the unknown trying to drown me. I started to see only one way out. I quit softball. Looking back now, I can see the truth of what happened, the true reason that I quit the sport that I loved and gave me so much joy. Satan was trying to steal my happiness, and I let him. Satan told me that I was not good enough to play with the other girls. He told me that I would fail and that it would be too hard. He spoke to the insecurities inside of me, put fear inside of me, and I let those insecurities and fear keep me from doing what I love. He made me afraid to step out and try something new so I would stay on my comfortable little island of safety. I had built this perfect little island of comfort for myself and Satan convinced me that is where I belong. He was turning my island of comfort into an island of isolation. We as Christians do not belong on islands. I wish I had clung onto Philippians 4:13 which says, "I can do all things through Christ who strengthens me." That is possibly one of the most quoted Bible verses, and I had heard it all my life growing up, but I let God's truth slip my mind, while I was allowing Satan's lies inside. I had pushed away God's peaceful, loving voice of truth to listen to Satan's lies. I was not looking to God for strength, so I fell short and continued down the path of listening to Satan's voice, instead of my loving Father's voice.

Having quit softball, I now had a lot of free time on my hands, but Stetson was still in baseball, so I was alone. It didn't take long for Satan to steal Stetson's joy as well and to further my dependence on him. He quit baseball. Satan convinced him that it would be more fun to party and live a life of sin than play baseball. With all this free time we now had, we made even more bad decisions. Satan was creating the perfect storm for destruction in our lives, and we were oblivious. I started partying and drinking more. I put little to no effort into my classes. Of course, I was almost always with Stetson, and he was making bad decisions as well. He started smoking pot. I was aware of it, but I chose to ignore it, hoping it would just go away. A terrible decision to make about any sin in your own life or a friend's life. Galatians 6:1 says, "Dear brothers and sisters, if another believer is overcome by some sin, you who are godly should gently and humbly help that person back onto the right path. And be careful not to fall into the same temptation yourself." God wants us to keep each other accountable, and to steer each other towards Him and His love for us. We cannot ignore the sins in each other's lives, for this is allowing each other to fail. We were called to live victorious lives, and lives filled with joy. We cannot be victorious if people around us are failing. We were created to help others and give them hope and encouragement. I chose to ignore instead of encourage, and therefore, Stetson continued on in his sin, and I was beginning to fall into more temptation. He never did it in front of me because he knew I hated it, so there were times when I was alone, and I did feel so alone. The fears of new people that Satan had put inside of me kept me from making friends. If I wasn't with Stetson, I had no one. I would hide away in my dorm room and wait for him. I was stranded on the island of isolation. Stetson was my foundation, but like I said, he was not a good foundation. I could see the cracks forming.

Then we started making bad decisions together, we became sexually active. The sad thing is that all these things we were doing were normal college culture. The world has deemed these sins normal and acceptable. Dear friend, do not let the world lie to you. The things that the world says is normal and fun to do, is Satan's way of imprisoning you. You become a slave to your sin. In John 8, Jesus is speaking to the Jews and he says, "You will know the truth, and the truth will set you free." (verse 32) The Jews become confused saying we "have never been slaves of anyone. How can you say that we shall be set free? Jesus replies, 'I tell you the truth, everyone who sins is a slave to sin.'" (verse 33-34) I was like the Jews. I was not even aware I was in bondage. I had closed my mind and heart off from the truth because I wanted to live to gratify my flesh. I had listened to Satan's lies that were telling me living this way would fulfill me. I was living moment to moment trying to feel good. Filling your life with worldly things will never fulfill you or give you joy. I can tell you now, that sin and the pleasures of this world can seem pleasurable for a while, but sin destroys all that is good. What I was doing felt fun and good, but my sinful ways were leading me into destruction.

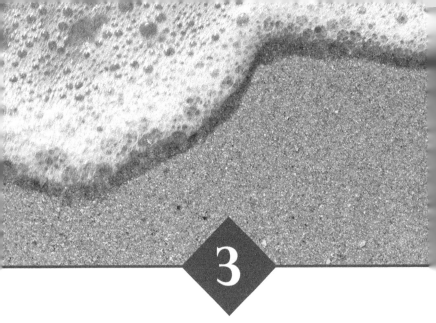

The Destruction

"You can enter God's Kingdom only through the narrow gate. The highway to hell is broad, and its gate is wide for the many who choose that way."

Matthew 7:13

My first semester went on like this, indulging my flesh and living in sin. I went from one party to the next. If I wasn't spending time with Stetson, I was depressed. I would drag myself from class to class, then hole up in my room waiting for him to come see me. He started hanging out with one of his friends more and more, smoking weed every day, leaving me alone. I just ignored it and tried to hold onto my cracked foundation. I thought I was living that great college life, and then reality hit the night before my last final. Stetson got pulled over and thrown in jail for possession of marijuana. The foundation of my island had crumbled with no one to save me. I was floating, isolated, with nowhere to go. I spent the night crying and wondering what in the world I was going to do. My boyfriend is in jail. For drugs. I am two hours from home, with no one to help me or care about me. I was scared and alone. The next morning, my dad calls me. He was literally the last person in the world I wanted to be talking to at that moment. He knew about what happened to Stetson. News travels fast in our tiny town, but something funny happened. He wasn't mad. He asked me if I was ok and if I needed anything. He didn't condemn me. He called to check on his baby girl. As easy as it would have been for him to say, "Of course he would do something like that" or "what are you doing with a guy like that?" he didn't. He extended love and compassion. Isn't that just like our Heavenly Father? No matter what situations we get ourselves into, no matter what hole we have dug for ourselves, God is not judgmental. He does not point out where we went wrong. He extends love and compassion. He loves us with a love that is so consuming that it forgets all wrongs. In Isaiah 43:25 the Lord says "'I, yes, I alone, will blot out your sins for my own sake and will never think of them again.'" The Lord knows your sins no more. He does not desire to condemn you but desires to show you his never-ending love and mercy. "But you, O Lord, are a God of compassion and mercy, slow to get angry and filled with unfailing love and faithfulness." Psalms 86:15. God was not angry with me, just like my earthly father was not.

They loved me. Through my dad, God was showing his compassion and mercy. I did not deserve it. I had made bad decision after bad decision and deliberately ignored things that I knew were bad. God still loved me. God still cared about me and He still showed me grace and compassion, because it did not matter how I came to that bad spot in my life; He still had grace and compassion for me because He loves me.

Stetson got out of jail later that night. I was just glad he was out of jail and safe, I didn't think about the repercussions of this, or what would happen afterward. Life went on with that ordeal in our rearview. He quit college and got a job in the oilfield around our hometown. I went back to college for my second semester, and I was still just floating. I had no idea what to do. I was living moment to moment. Stetson was not there with me and I had no friends there because I had spent all my time with him, the center of my world. I would quietly go to class, and then quickly come back to my dorm room and sleep all day. I fell into a depression. My island of isolation was floating away. I would come back to Leedey every weekend to see Stetson and he would also come see me during the week at times. In between visits, I was depressed. I had no one. I remember one particular weekend, my mom could tell that something was wrong and tried to talk to me, asking how college was. I crumbled and told her I had no friends and felt so lonely at college. My depression was taking me deeper and I did not know how to get out of it. My sweet mother prayed with me that I would find Godly friends and seek Him. If only I would have realized that I had the only friend I would ever need, and He was always very near. Jesus Christ. Who if not the

One who was despised and rejected while on earth could have identified with me more? I was seeking for a human to make me feel less lonely and depressed, but Jesus is the only One who can fill that need. Jesus is the only one that can make us feel whole. Dear friend, if you feel lonely and rejected, seek Jesus. Pick up God's word and breathe it in. Isaiah 41:9 says, "I have called you back from the ends of the earth, saying, 'You are my servant.' *For I have chosen you and will not throw you away."* You are *chosen.* God sees you because He is with you. Seek God and you will find Him. Draw near to Him and He will draw near to you for He loves you.

That semester ended with frequent trips to see Stetson and not much gained. I had barely passed my classes and was just glad I was able to go back home, where I felt slightly more secure. Stetson had been working and doing drugs while I was gone. I didn't know it at the time, but he had started doing cocaine along with marijuana to survive the oilfield life. While Satan was pushing me further into isolation, he was pulling him further into drugs. We were both caught in a world of sin and did not even realize it. Satan loves to make us sin, but he loves it even more when we are blind to it. He wants us to be spiritually blind. Blind to his lies, blind to his deceit and destruction, but most importantly, blind to God and His love. 2 Corinthians 4:4 says "Satan, who is the god of this world, has blinded the minds of those who don't believe. They are unable to see the glorious light of the Good News. They don't understand this message about the glory of Christ, who is the exact likeness of God." I was being blinded so I couldn't see my Savior and His Glorious Light. I was in darkness, brought on by Satan. He had so blinded me, I did not even realize how miserable I was. He was blinding me from the truth of how depressed and unhappy I was. But when I was with Stetson, it all seemed to be better for a while. Until I realized I was pregnant.

19 years old, no job, no college degree, not married, and carrying a child. I felt more lost than ever. Telling my parents was one of the hardest things I have ever had to do. I knew I couldn't keep it from them forever, but I was so scared to disappoint them even further. When I told them, they were disappointed, but they made sure I knew that they loved me. I knew this is not what they wanted for my life. I knew they were disappointed in me. I was starting to even disappoint myself, but I was isolated and lost, not knowing how to change. I could see my life going down a dangerous path, but I had no idea how to stop it. I was ashamed of what my brother and sister would think as well. I felt like the black sheep of the family, making mistake after mistake. But each of them reached out to me saying they loved me. They cared for me, even after all my mistakes. Many tears later, we started preparing for the baby. I was never a baby person. I never had an interest in children. I was the youngest of my siblings, hardly any of my friends had younger siblings, and therefore, I had zero experience with babies and children. I had no idea how to take care of a baby and neither did Stetson, but he was excited to be a dad. However, he was still partying and doing drugs, and I was still ignoring it.

I worked in a café over the summer and decided to drop out of college. I did not want to be the pregnant, unmarried girl walking around campus. I also had no idea what I wanted to become or work for, so I had no desire to go back anyway. I didn't know what I was going to do. I was in shock and filled with shame. Shame walked around with me daily, kept my head low and my heart filled with sadness. While I never exactly knew what I wanted to do with my life, I knew that this was not it. Looking back, I know that shame kept me from coming to God and asking Him to help me and forgive me. Shame is a shackle that keeps our hands bound from reaching out to God. Shame puts chains around our legs that keep us from walking towards the life that God has for us. Shame kept me on that island of isolation that Satan pushed me on to. Dear friends, if you are suffering from shame, that is a lie from Satan. Romans 8:1 says "there is no condemnation for those who belong to Christ Jesus." God does not condemn you for your actions, for your words, or for things that have been done to you. You belong to God. He did not create you to carry the burdens of your past. He created you to be free and live your life joyfully for Him. Isaiah 54:4 is such a comforting verse for me because it states "Fear not; you will no longer live in shame. Don't be afraid; there is no more disgrace for you. You will no longer remember the shame of your youth …" I am not what the world said I was and what Satan told me I was. Unwed mother. Pregnant teen. Lost and broken. Unable. Useless. Hopeless. These labels came from the father of lies, Satan. I was more than a label. You are more than a label. There is no disgrace for us in Jesus Christ. He came to die on this Earth so that we could be free from disgrace, shame, and labels. He carried those things to the cross and was crucified with them. Do not go on carrying them around! They were died and buried with Jesus so that you may live freely! Satan does not get to label us because he did not create us. Our

21

Creator gives us our name and it is Loved Child of God. God created us and calls us redeemed, cleansed, holy, and a new creation. I pray that you will grab onto this today and live in the freeness that Jesus paid for. I pray that you will slough off the shackles of sin and shame and live free. "So if the Son sets you free, you are truly free." John 8:36.

Stetson lived by himself while I lived with my parents. He still worked in the oilfield and worked long hours. He was either working or partying. I saw him very little and began to feel even more isolated. I began to feel that he did not care about me and what I was going through. He was choosing his friends and partying over me. I was not feeling so chosen by him anymore, but I did not know how to change it. We had begun the life of living worldly by partying and gratifying our flesh, and Satan was telling Stetson this is what he should do. Stetson was trapped by the drugs and drinking. They were taking him down a dark path that is not easy to come back from. I knew none of this, so I merely thought he did not want to be with me anymore. Satan was lying to me as well. I was pregnant, alone, and scared. Having a baby is a happy, exciting time for most people. For me, it was shame-filled and depressing. I did not want to talk about having the baby, because the circumstances were not happy. I did not want to think about what would happen when I had the baby, because I did not know what would happen. I did not know if Stetson would quit his wild ways to take care of me and the baby. I did not know what my life would look like. I couldn't imagine having a good future after such a failure, so I didn't look forward. I just survived. I lived day by day in this shameful life. Shame was surrounding me. I was a pregnant teen, living with my parents while my boyfriend partied. I was embarrassed to go anywhere (besides to fulfill my pizza pregnancy cravings), and I was ashamed to be seen.

Then, the time came to have the baby and I was even more scared. I called Stetson to come take me to the hospital so we could have our baby. A few short hours later and there she was. Laid on my chest, the cutest little face I had ever seen. I was terrified, but also numb (and not just from the epidural). This baby was mine to take care of. If I had known at the time what a blessing this little baby would be, I would have cried with joy and praised God. Instead, I cried from shame and fear, and let Satan lie to me more. I loved this baby, but I was ashamed of the way she came to be. I was ashamed that my life did not look picture perfect. I was ashamed that I had become another girl that got knocked up by her boyfriend. I loved her, but I was ashamed of her because of my sins. I was not a proud mother, showing off her baby. I was hiding due to shame that Satan was piling on me. Thankfully, my Lord was not ashamed of me, or my beautiful daughter. God is never ashamed of us, no matter what we think of ourselves or what the world thinks of us. Jesus brought us into our salvation when he died on the cross, so he made us equals with himself. Hebrews 2:10-11 says, "God, for whom and through whom everything was made, chose to bring many children into glory. And it was only right that he should make Jesus, through his suffering, a perfect leader, fit to bring them into their salvation. So now Jesus and the ones he makes holy have the same Father. That is why Jesus is not ashamed to call them his brothers and sisters." God *chose us.* He *chose* to bring us into his glory knowing that we were sinners, knowing that we could not be holy the way that He is holy. He is not ashamed of us because he *chose* to have us share in His glory and have us share a relationship with His Holy Son. The shame and disgrace I was feeling were not coming from my Savior who chose me, but from Satan who was trying to steal me from God and destroy me. My God was not ashamed of me; if only I had seen that.

Later that night after delivering sweet little Lynlee Elaine, Stetson went back home. He did not come back until the next night to take me home. I found out years later he was out doing cocaine. I thought I knew what isolation felt like, but that night I really knew. I was in the hospital, trying to take care of a baby that was suddenly mine, all by myself. I had no clue what I was doing. I was in survival mode. My island of isolation and shame was pushed further away. A fog of confusion and fear enveloped me, and I didn't know where to turn or what to do. I brought Lynlee home to my parents' house, not knowing what the future held. I was just trying to keep this baby alive and not mess up my life even more. Looking back on this young version of myself, my heart aches for her. My heart aches for the pain she has already endured and for the pain that is coming her way. I sometimes wonder what my life would be like if I would have surrendered to God at this point; if I would have cried out to God and asked Him to turn my life around. He would have been there in an instant because He never left me. He was always there, watching me, waiting for me to reach towards Him and His love. He hurt for me just like I was hurting. He longed to take away my suffering, but He knew if He did, I would not have become fully developed. So, He lovingly allowed me to continue down the road of suffering and heartache; and I continued down the road of destruction unknowingly.

The few days after having Lynlee, Stetson asked me to move in with him. I did not feel this was the right thing to do, but I did it anyway. He also gave me a ring, an engagement ring. It was his grandmothers and it was beautiful. He loved me and wanted to marry me. I loved him too, but as much as we loved each other, we couldn't discuss marriage. We both knew deep down that we were not in a place to get married. I could not make myself even imagine getting married while being filled with so much shame. I loved Stetson, and I longed to feel better, secure, and I thought just moving in with him might be the way. Oh how wrong I was. I had listened to Satan's lies for so long, I didn't know what the truth was. I didn't know *who* the truth was. I couldn't see the truth through the lies I had been believing. I had long ago abandoned the teachings that my mother had laid in my heart. My mom and dad were devastated by my decision. Little did they know, that I was devastated as well. I could not see through the fog. I could not see that my decisions were taking me deeper and deeper. Stetson and I were living lives of sin and deceit, and Satan had succeeded in blinding us from that realization. I was living life to feel better. I felt shame and condemnation for getting pregnant before I was married. I was ashamed of how my family was growing. It was not the picture-perfect family that most people have. My family was starting from sin and shame, and Satan whispered that I was damaged. He told me that my life was ruined, worthless, and disgraceful. I let Satan make me feel that way, even though I longed to not feel that way. I longed to feel value. I was still longing to feel *chosen*. What I was truly longing for, was the love of Christ. But I was not listening to His quiet, still voice that tells me I do have value and that I am chosen. I listened to Satan's lies because I was being a child of the father that I was following. Jesus states in John 8:44-45, "'For you are the children of your father the devil, and you love to do the evil things he does. He was a murderer from the beginning. He has always hated the truth, because there is no truth in him. When he lies, it is consistent with his character; for he is a liar and the father of lies. So when I tell the truth, you just naturally don't believe me!'" I was allowing Satan to be my father, and I was allowing his lies to determine who I thought I was. Jesus said Satan is the father of lies, and that is what he was being to me. I wasn't listening to my true Father's voice, so I was not believing the truths He was telling me. Satan does not get to determine who we are. He does not get to tell us that our family is not good enough. God blesses what He loves, and God loved me. God loved Stetson and He wanted to bless us. It did not matter how we started our family, and it did not matter what Satan and the world said about us. Dear friend, it does not matter what the world says about you, and it does not matter what Satan has said about you. You have value because the Holy Creator made you. In Genesis 1:27 it says that "God created human beings in his own image." We are the image of God, the Holiest of Holies, the Divine Lord. Therefore, we have value which comes from our Creator. But I could not hear God's truth, I could not hear how valued I was, because I had forsaken it and ignored His voice, so I clung onto Satan's lies. I kept believing that I was ruined and that my family was a disgrace. I was caught in Satan's web of lies, death, and destruction that ultimately leaves you in a pit of despair.

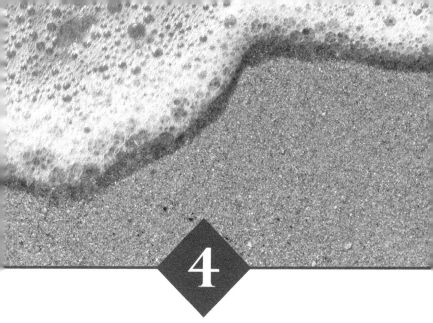

4

The Pit

"You intended to harm me, but God intended it all for good. He brought me to this position so I could save the lives of many people."

Genesis 50:20

My little island had shrunk even more. By moving in with Stetson I had hurt my parents and caused a rift between us. They still loved me, but something had changed. I couldn't bear to talk to them or see them for fear of the shame I would feel. I could not stand to see the disappointment on their faces and their sadness for me. I felt shame and condemnation at every turn. While my relationship with my parents had changed, my whole life had also changed. Stetson would go to work and I would stay home with Lynlee. She was the bright spot in a very dark fog. I loved spending time with her and taking care of her. I loved to go outside and enjoy the sunshine with her, take afternoon naps with her on the couch, and rock her to sleep each night. She was a sweet child who brought me much joy during that dark time. She was my saving grace, my little angel sent from God. While Stetson worked long hours, he also partied. He would go to work during the day, then go to parties most nights. I would call him over and over again asking when he was coming home. When he was home, I never felt like he wanted to be there. Yes, he was always a guy on the move, but his heart never seemed like it was at home with us. Satan is a deceiver. Satan had deceived me into filling myself up with worldly things and he did the same to Stetson. He did not have the desire to be with us because his desire lied in the world due to Satan's deception. Satan was putting a fear inside of him to keep him from his blessings. He did not want him to have a family, to feel the love of a daughter. I can look back and see how torn Stetson was, between what he wanted, and what Satan told him to do. Satan told him that he was not good enough to be with us. As Stetson fell further and further into the party scene, Satan convinced him that that is where he belonged. He convinced him that he did not deserve good things and that he was a failure. As Satan was stealing his blessings, he began to steal our happiness. The Stetson that I moved in with was not the boy that I met in high school. He did not want to spend time with me anymore, and he was not as kind to me anymore. Something had drastically changed, but I was too blind and numb to know what it was. I was letting the shame and disgrace that I felt blind me. Satan convinced me that I did not deserve better either. Since my family had started so disgracefully, I did not deserve happiness. But God tells us we do deserve those things. "But God is so rich in mercy, and he loved us so much, that even though we were dead because of our sins, he gave us life when he raised Christ from the dead. (It is only by God's grace that you have been saved!)" Ephesians 2:4-5. Because of God's love for us, I did deserve happiness, I did deserve love. God does not care where we come from, what we have done, or who we are. God is rich in mercy, He loves us, and wants to give us *life*. Satan had made me spiritually blind, so I could not see this. Due to my blindness, I allowed him to steal everything I had.

As time went on, Stetson would be gone more than a day at a time. I would ask him where he had been, and he always seemed to have some excuse. He was out with this person and they ran out of gas, he was too tired so he just stopped and slept. I grew tired of the excuses, and tired of ragging on him all the time. I became exhausted from trying to figure out why he did not want to be home with me. I was exhausted from thinking about what happened to the sweet boy I used to know. My life had changed so fast and I wasn't sure what to do. I didn't know what to say or what to think about it, so I just shut it off. I shut off trying to figure it all out. I shut off wondering why he seemed so different than he used to be. I let Satan push my island of isolation further into the fog of fear and confusion. The fog kept me from seeing that Stetson was falling deeper into drugs. He had fallen into methamphetamines. This drug has been called "The Devil's Drug" and I firmly believe it is. Meth was a word that I thought would never have anything to do with me or anyone I knew. But Satan is so full of lies and deceit, and is so desperate to destroy anyone that he will tear down their defenses until something that used to be despicable to them now seems ok. This drug infiltrates the users mind and creates chaos and confusion. Imagine that every thought that enters your head is born from hate and paranoia. Your mind becomes a playground for evil spirits. Again, I was blind to the fact that this is what Stetson was doing. I was blind to the fact that Satan had him in his clutches. I was so caught up in my shame and loneliness that I couldn't see the truth.

When Lynlee was almost a year old I got a job because Stetson could not hold down a job for long. He had quit the oilfield job and tried multiple jobs after that. Satan and the drugs that had trapped him were destroying every relationship he had, so everyone that offered him a job eventually fired him due to his actions. He would get a good job, and two days later say he quit or was fired. I was so angry and frustrated, but I just shut down. I didn't know what to do, and I couldn't control the situation. It had spiraled out of my control. I couldn't force him to get a job and keep it. So I just went with the flow. I went to my job and took care of Lynlee. I let Stetson do whatever and did my own thing. This is a dangerous way to live. I was not taking charge of my life and I was not taking care of my family. I was letting Satan direct where my life was going. I couldn't control it so I just let go. But I should have let *God take control.* I surrendered control, but not to the Holy One. I surrendered to the will of the world and it took me deeper into a pit. While I had shut off the questions, Stetson began to question me. He began to always ask where I was, what I was doing, who I was talking to. Every answer I gave him was frustrating for him and he began to not believe me. I would get so frustrated trying to answer every question he had for me. I was becoming filled with anger, but I couldn't show it. My anger would only make him angry. When he would get angry, he would yell or leave and I would not see him for days.

I began to live life by merely trying not to provoke Stetson. I didn't want him to ask me anymore questions or accuse me of anything else. So I tried not to go anywhere but work. I tried not to talk to any more people than I had to. At work, I made sure I didn't say anything to anybody that would make him question me. I was living life in fear and letting fear guide me. Oh how I wish I had clung onto Joshua 1:9. "This is my command-be strong and courageous! Do not be afraid or discouraged. For the Lord your God is with you wherever you go." I was filled with fear and so discouraged from what I had allowed Satan to do in my life. Dear friend, if you are in a position like this, be strong and courageous! God is with you and will never leave you. Do not allow Satan to guide you through fear and intimidation. Seek God and His will for your life. "Don't be afraid, for I am with you. Don't be discouraged, for I am your God. I will strengthen you and help you. I will hold you up with my victorious right hand." Isaiah 41:10. God is a good, loving God who desires to strengthen us.

By living in fear, I was thrust further into the fog, further into isolation. The inquisitions were endless and exhausting. Satan's drug was putting paranoia about every little thing into Stetson's mind. He began waking me up in the middle of the night asking me insane questions. I had to have answers to everything he asked about or he would become angry. When he first started doing this, I was so confused as to why all these little things he asked about were so important, especially in the middle of the night. With Satan's drug and its hate and paranoia infiltrating Stetson's mind, everything that he saw or heard was questionable. Why does the car have less gas than last time, where did this piece of paper in the trash come from, why were you in my pickup, why, why, why. I could never answer his questions the way he wanted. Every answer I gave was wrong and just led to more questions, and he never believed me anyway. Satan would whisper that I was lying until that is all Stetson could think. These late night arguments became normal, until I no longer was confused about them. I just wanted them to stop. I just wanted him to shut up long enough so that I could go to sleep. So I would just try to not make him angrier. I was so lonely on my island and the fog of confusion was so thick that I couldn't see what was wrong with him, so I stopped wondering. I just tried to survive.

He would call me at work asking wild and crazy things, and I would have to turn around to help customers, acting like my life was cupcakes and rainbows. One day at work he called me and told me to come outside. When I got outside, he was out there ready to fight. He ranted on about everything he could find wrong with me. I was crying, asking him to stop until he finally sped off and left. He tore me to pieces, and I had to pick them all up to try and finish my day of work. I wore a fake smile every day and tried not to let anyone see my pain. My normal day was feeling depressed, alone, and exhausted inside while trying to help others with a fake smile. I am sure so many people can relate to this. This is not how I wanted to live, and this is not how God wanted or planned for me to live. God created us to live abundant and victorious lives, and lives filled with the Holy Spirit. 1 Corinthians 15:57 says, "But thank God! He gives us victory over sin and death through our Lord Jesus Christ." He has given us victory to live in! He desires us to live in that victory and to share in His glory! My days of living defeated were not only hurting me but also God because He did not create me to live that life. He was awaiting the day that I would wake up and grab onto the victory that Jesus Christ won for us!

God also created us to love and live in harmony with others. Not only was my isolation keeping me from God, but it was also keeping me from reaching out to others. Ecclesiastes 4:9-10 says "Two people are better off than one, for they can help each other succeed. If one person falls, the other can reach out and help. But someone who falls alone is in real trouble." I was falling alone, and I was in real trouble. I had fallen away from God and from people. I worked with some wonderful, God-loving ladies, and I know that if I had asked for help or prayer, they would not have hesitated to support me and love me. I know that if I had reached out to my parents and asked for help, they would been there in an instant. This is the call of Christ, to reach out and help one another. Verse 12 continues saying "A person standing alone can be attacked and defeated, but two can stand back-to-back and conquer. Three are even better, for a triple-braided cord is not easily broken." I was being attacked and defeated because Satan had made me isolated. His lies and deceit had isolated me and kept me from people. He brought me to an island all alone and was preparing to strand me there. He isolated me; therefore he was winning this fight. If you are feeling isolated, broken, defeated, or just barely making it through life, reach out. Reach out to God to lift you up. Reach out to someone who will pray for you and help you bear your burdens. This is the triple-braided cord. Another person, standing back-to-back with you asking God for mercy and deliverance. Two people and a Heavenly Father conquering the enemy. We cannot do it alone and we cannot bear our burdens alone. Galatians 6:2 tells us to "share each other's burdens, and in this way obey the law of Christ." I was too full of shame to ask someone to share the burden with me, but that was Satan lying to me to keep me on my island of isolation. He wanted me scared and alone so that I would not reach out to God. And it worked, so on my island I continued to stay.

Two times I was woken up to a phone call in the middle of the night saying that Stetson had been pulled over for drunk driving and was thrown in jail. The first time I went and bailed him out. I did not want him to rot in jail, even if it was his fault. I wanted him to know that I loved him no matter what and that I would never condemn him for his actions. I remember feeling a sorrow for him. I could feel the sorrow for his actions that he was feeling, but not showing. I wanted to show him that I loved him no matter what. Before I bailed him out, I went and bought him a wedding ring. Even though our lives were chaos, and even though I doubted his love for me at times, I still knew deep down that I loved him. I knew that I wanted to spend my life with him. Somehow, someway, I was showing him the grace of God. I was so worn out and tired from Stetson's shenanigans, but I could not abandon him and leave him alone. I know now that God was guiding me to give Stetson grace because that is what he needed to survive. I know now that when I looked at Stetson, what I saw was a scared and lonely soul, just like I was. I wanted him to be ok, I just did not know how to help him yet. I couldn't even help myself. But God knew. God helped me to show Stetson grace and love. Even though I was far from God, He was not far from me. Hebrews 13:5 says "God has said, 'Never will I leave you; never will I forsake you.'" Even though we were in a pit, even though we put ourselves there with our sins, God did not forsake us. God created Stetson and I to be together. God put the love for each other in our hearts and nothing could remove it. He was renewing it and deepening even through the pain. I was isolated on my island while Stetson was isolated in his hurricane. I was hurt, but I could not stand to see Stetson hurt either. I gave him the ring to show him I loved him. He told me he loved me too, but we both knew we were still not ready to get married. Things still were hard and chaotic between us, but we loved each other. So, I bailed him out the second time he got a DUI as well. It was a few months later after many fights, arguments, and late night inquisitions. I was not as graceful about it this time, but I still didn't have the heart to abandon him. I couldn't bear to let him feel isolated and abandoned the way that I felt. I knew how that felt, and I could not stand the thought of Stetson feeling that way. I loved him too much to let him feel isolated.

One day, I decided to try to reach out and spend some time with my friends. I wasn't ready to ask for help, but I did want to try and feel some normalcy. That night was anything but normal. Stetson called me all night wondering who I was with, where I was, what I was doing. I couldn't focus or have fun. My friends tried to tell me in the nicest way possible that Stetson was not the right guy for me. I didn't know what to tell them because I didn't know if he was either, anymore. I still felt love for him, but the hurt was becoming too much. I was so lost, alone, and surrounded by Satan's lies that I didn't know what was right for me anymore. Satan had so confused me and isolated me that I didn't know how abnormal and chaotic my life had become. The fog had so enveloped me that I could not determine right from wrong. When I arrived home that night, Stetson questioned me endlessly. He didn't believe a word that I told him. He was convinced that I was lying to him and deceiving him. This was the first night that I realized how much Stetson had changed. The questions about that night lasted for months and months. Satan used that night and Stetsons confused mind to fuel his paranoia. Satan poured lie after lie into his mind about me. He did not trust me, and he did not believe me. He was convinced that I was doing despicable things. Satan told him that every word I said and that everything I did was despicable. Satan made him believe that I was lying to him and deceiving him. He questioned me over and over about that night, and I began to feel helpless. Nothing that I said could change his mind. I began to question myself. Maybe I was doing something wrong? Maybe I was deceiving Stetson in some way? The craziness of all the questions began to make me feel crazy. No matter what I said or did, it was never enough to convince Stetson that I was telling the truth. Satan was pointing the blame at me so that Stetson would not see that Satan was the real deceiver. This is what Satan does. He makes us focus on people and what they have done to us, instead of realizing that Satan is the one that has been the destroyer all along. Satan was robbing both of us of a loving and trusting relationship. I loved Stetson deeply, but he was not the fun-loving guy that I first met. He was not so happy and full of life like I remembered. He had become perpetually angry and paranoid. I never thought to question why he had changed so drastically. I never really understood that Stetson was deep into drugs. Now, I see God's hand everywhere in this story. God lovingly used the fog around me to protect me. While Satan was using the fog to confuse and isolate me further, God was using it for my protection. Genesis 50:20 says "You intended to harm me, but God intended it all for good." God used this suppressive cloud for my good because he loved me. God never left me nor forsake me. God closed off my mind from wondering what was going on and trying to understand, to just surviving. God is our protector, a shield around us. God was shielding me from the truth. The truth was that Stetson was falling deeper into the world of drugs, and Satan was trying to drown him there. Had I known the truth and the full extent of what Stetson was doing, I would have left, and caused both of us to be more broken than we already were. We were both broken people trying to survive. But God does not want us *just* to survive. He wants us to have an abundant life. John 10:10 says, "The thief's purpose is to steal and kill and destroy. My purpose is to give them a rich and satisfying life." Satan was stealing everything from us, he was killing our relationship, and destroying everything around us. But God's purpose is to give us an abundant life. Satan was trying to harm us, but God was going to use it for our good, to give us an abundant life. God cares about us too much to let us not come to completion. Had I left Stetson, I would have not come to find God and had a full life renewal. Stetson would not have been redeemed and renewed as well. God used the fog to protect us and prepare us for the future. He used all the moments of torment for our good, to strengthen us for the future.

Stetson told me one night that he had tried meth. I did not know what to say, but I hoped that he would not try it again. As I said, I did not know the things that were going on and I thank God every day that I didn't. What he didn't tell me, is that he had been using it every day. He was caught up in a hurricane of drugs and deceit. Stetson was so hurt from everything he had done, and Satan was whispering that it would not get better. Satan told him to look at the pain he had caused and convinced him that he could not do better. He convinced Stetson that the drugs were the only thing that was there for him. He told him that all he does is cause pain and heartache, and there was nothing he could do about it. Stetson felt hopeless and defeated from all the lies and hate that Satan was pouring on him. Satan was pushing him further into the pit, hoping to destroy him. He was pitting us against each other. He was poisoning his mind with hate and lies. I was moving through a fog trying to survive the arguments and the hopelessness. Our lives were miserable. We were not wrestling with each other, though. We were wrestling with Satan. Satan was trying to destroy us. He was using everything he could against us. He turned us against each other. Ephesians 6:12 says, "For we are not fighting against flesh-and-blood enemies, but against evil rulers and authorities of the unseen world, against mighty powers in this dark world, and against evil spirits in the heavenly places." Satan was using drugs as an evil ruler, and this evil ruler was ruling Stetson. Through this evil ruler, he was ruining lives. We were wrestling against Satan and his evil spirits. Regardless, God was there at every moment. Had we only looked for Him, we would have found him. God never left us to wrestle by ourselves. He knew the outcome of our wrestling, and He knew that this fight was making us stronger.

Every time Stetson left, I was filled with relief that he was gone and a fear of what would happen to him. He drove recklessly, fueled by rage and anger. I never knew each time if that would be the last time that I would see him. When he would come back, I would feel relief that he was safe and alive, quickly followed by dread, anger, and hurt due to the things he would say and do. He would bust in the house with new paranoias each day and new lies from Satan. He would be gone days at a time. I would call him and call him with no answer. I would fear the worst had happened, and then he would come back and the vicious cycle of arguments and fights would start again. He left in rage one time and I did not see him again until two days later. I tried to call him over and over again but his phone was dead. When he came back, he kicked the door down. I could see the hysteria in his eyes. He yelled at me, telling me that he had been wandering around a canyon because one of his friends he did drugs with left him there. I was speechless. He was so angry for being left there, and I was so confused. I couldn't tell if he was telling me the truth or if this was another ploy to get me to feel sorry for him. I fell into the pattern I was accustomed to at that point, I just nodded and tried to placate him. All I could do was try not to anger him further until he would eventually leave or fall asleep. But sleep did not come easily. Meth is a drug that stimulates your brain so Stetson rarely slept. When he did sleep, it was fitful and honestly scary. He would grind his teeth, his heart would race, and his breathing wavered from extremely slow to scarily fast. When he slept, I could barely sleep as well because I feared that his heart would give out. When I did finally fall asleep, I would be woken again with a new round of questions. And then another fight would start.

The fights were horrible. Nothing I did could fix them or make them stop so I just yelled and screamed for Stetson to stop. I cried and begged him to leave me alone, but the drugs, those evil rulers, were pouring so much confusion and hate into him. If I wasn't yelling, asking him to stop, I was quiet and calm to try to calm him. But nothing worked. Stetson would throw things, kick things, and tear things up. He never hurt me or tried to, because his anger was not directed towards me. He was hurt from what Satan was doing to him and angry at everything due to the hate and anger Satan was putting inside of him. He was trying to destroy Stetson and me along with him. I was never physically hurt, but I was mentally and emotionally hurt every day. During the fights I would try to get away from him, but there was nowhere to go. If I shut a door, he would kick it down. I began going to our closet because it was the smallest room and I felt that I could somehow hide in there. He began to accuse me of putting cameras in there to video him. The paranoia was overwhelming and the accusations that were flung at me were emotionally killing me. The yelling and torment each day were mentally overwhelming me. The endless fighting, the endless accusing, and the endless chaos was mentally and emotionally draining. I did not know how to handle my emotions anymore. We would argue, going around and around for hours every night. He would accuse me of this and that and not hear a word I said in refute. You cannot reason with a person on drugs. The miraculous thing throughout all of this chaotic time is that Lynlee slept peacefully through every fight, argument, and yelling match we had. She never woke up or cried out. Though Stetson and I's life was nothing but grief and turmoil, Lynlee knew nothing but love and peace. God was not only keeping Stetson and me safe through everything, but His arms were always around our sweet baby.

Due to my very little sleep, and the emotional and mental exhaustion, I was a nervous and anxious wreck. I became paranoid as well, always checking my actions and behavior, hoping I had not done anything that would cause Stetson to ask questions. But everything I did was wrong. Every move I made, no matter how innocuous, was questioned and picked apart. I would make an innocent remark about the weather and he would focus on it for days, wondering why I said that. I would look at one spot on the wall too long and he would assume there were hidden cameras there. The paranoia was exhausting. I was scared to go anywhere, even the grocery store, for fear of another accusation or another month-long fight about where I was going. I did not want to see anyone for fear that they might ask me anything or tell me they saw Stetson doing something he wasn't supposed to. I was in constant fear of something bad happening or being said to me. Stetson accompanied me to the grocery store one time. I saw someone I knew and asked them a simple question. Afterward, Stetson told me I had treated that lady horribly, and that I was an awful person. He tried to berate me and drag me down for everything I did on that simple trip to the store. Satan would not allow us to have a normal day, much less a normal minute. I can see now that Satan was heaping accusations on Stetson daily, and therefore made Stetson heap them onto me. Satan made Stetson feel awful, so Stetson made me feel awful as well. Every little thing I did or said was questioned. It was frustrating and exhausting. Finding the energy to live and breathe each day was a struggle. I was worn down from trying to survive each day and the arguments every night. I was depressed, lonely, and destroyed inside. My soul was crushed from the weight of everything Satan was piling on me. I went from not being able to control my emotions, to having no emotions. I was too tired for emotions. I was exhausted and numb. I let the fog of confusion envelop me even more. I kept going for Lynlee because she needed me. She kept me sane during these awful times. Her smiling face, and her sweet baby hands kept me grounded and gave me something to fight for.

Meanwhile, I could see the frustration building up in Stetson. Nothing I could ever say or do made him calm down or at ease. The hurricane of drugs was dragging him in and destroying everything around him. He was helpless and lost. He was growing angrier and angrier, at himself, at the situation around him, and at the pain he was causing. It came to the sad point that I almost hoped he would die so he would be at peace. I found myself hoping he would not return home each time, that something would happen. This was a hard realization to have. Every time that he came back home, I had almost wished he hadn't returned. I almost wished that he had died so that he would not be so hurt and in turmoil all the time. It was painful for me to see the man I loved in so much pain with no way to help them. He threatened to kill himself one time, and I remember feeling nothing. I had no reaction. I didn't know what to say because I thought that it might be the end of this chaos. I knew that would bring us both peace, something that we had been lacking for so long. This was the hopelessness that I felt. We both did not have any desire to live the lives we were living any longer, but we were unable to do anything to fix it. We were two lost souls living lives of despair and anguish. We were helpless and broken with no way out that we could see. But God had a way out ready and was waiting for us to reach for it.

It was so hard to see the person that I loved in such turmoil and anger and have no idea how to help them. Feeling so helpless and shameful, I made my little island of loneliness and isolation even smaller. I stopped talking to my friends. I feared what they would say if they found out what my life was like. I couldn't imagine disturbing their fun college days with my life of misery. I was ashamed. It was easier to retreat to my island than ask someone to help me. Shame was my only friend on the island. Shame is a hateful friend. Shame kept me from reaching out because my shame was too heavy for me to bear. My eyes were downcast, and my head was bent from the weight of shame that Satan was heaping on me daily. I was bearing the burdens of my past sins, of the shame I felt from what Stetson was doing, the shame I felt from knowing that my life was hopeless. I was bearing burdens too heavy for me to carry alone, and Satan convinced me that this was how I was to live. But God did not create us to bear burdens. God sent His one and only Son to the cross so we would not have to bear these burdens. "Jesus said, 'Come to me, all of you who are weary and carry heavy burdens, and I will give you rest. Take my yoke upon you. Let me teach you, because I am humble and gentle at heart, and you will find rest for your soul. For my yoke is easy to bear, and the burden I give you is light.'" Matthew 11:28-30. Jesus took our burdens from us when he was hanging on the cross. I did not have to live that burdened life of shame because Jesus died to save me from that life. We do not have to live burdened lives, because Jesus became our sinful burden, and gave us His burden, which is to share the glorious love of God. God did not intend us to take on any burden alone. Not only did He give us Jesus to take our burdens, but He commanded each of us to help each other in our burdens. Galatians 6:2 says, "Share each other's burdens, and in this way obey the law of Christ." God commanded us to love one another and to share in each other's burdens because Jesus Christ did the same for us.

I remember after one day of nasty fights, Stetson left in a rage and I was left in pieces. I did the best thing I could have done, something I should have done long ago. I picked up my Bible. I didn't know what to read, but God was there guiding my hand. I turned to Psalms 69 and started reading at verse 14. "Rescue me from the mire, do not let me sink; deliver me from those who hate me, from the deep waters. Do not let the floodwaters engulf me or the depths swallow me up or the pit close its mouth over me. Answer me, O

Lord, out of the goodness of your love; in your great mercy turn to me." God is so good. His face was shining on me. He did not let the pit close its mouth over me. I read those verses over and over. I began to cry, wondering if these words could be for me. I wondered if God could still hear me after all this time of turning my back on Him and His love. This was my first step towards redemption. I was not too far gone. Dear friend, whatever you have done, or whatever struggle you find yourself in, *you are not too far gone.* There is no pit too dark or too deep that God cannot reach you. Even if you dug this pit yourself. God sees you. He will not let the pit close its mouth on you because He has great mercy. In Isaiah 45:7 God says "I create the light and make the darkness. I send good times and bad times. I, the Lord, am the one who does these things." God knows your struggle and he sees your pain. He is not leaving you abandoned. He knows where you are and will not leave you or forsake you. In this pit of darkness, God stretched out His hand and answered me, out of the goodness of His love. However, I was not immediately changed, and the fog around my island of grief, shame, despair, and condemnation did not lift. But the sun did start shining through. God gave me a glimpse of hope.

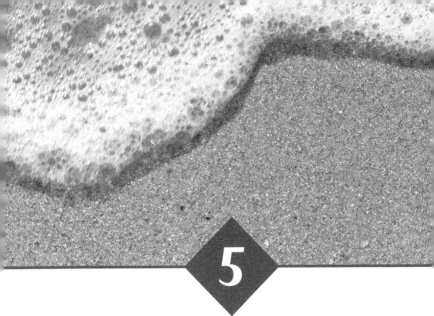

5

The Ascent

"Come, let us return to the Lord. He has torn us to pieces; now he will heal us. He has injured us; now he will bandage our wounds. In just a short time he will restore us, so that we may live in his presence."

Hosea 6:1-2

The glimpse of hope did not last long, because I did not grab hold of it. I should have been clinging to it like a life preserver, but I wasn't. I stayed on my island of isolation and let the fog envelop me again. I was so used to my island and the fog; I was afraid of hope and what it could bring. Satan kept me afraid of the unknown, so I would not try to change my life. When Satan puts us on an island, he determines to keep us there using any method he can. The unknown scared me, so I stayed miserable where I was. Shame had kept me from reaching out for help, so I stayed defeated where I was. I let Satan imprison me, and I allowed him keep me there. Thankfully, my God is a chain breaker. My God is a God of freedom and redemption. God was awaiting my day of freedom with patience and understanding. God understands and knows the perfect time. God looks at our lives and the lives around us eternally. Each moment we are in captivity or bondage is a trial to learn from. James 1:2-4 says "Dear brothers and sisters, when troubles of any kind come your way, consider it an opportunity for great joy. For you know that when your faith is tested, your endurance has a chance to grow. So let it grow, for when your endurance is fully developed, you will be perfect and complete, needing nothing." I know that God could not save me until my endurance was fully developed, until I was complete. Not only for my good but for the good of my family. I needed endurance to take care of my family, and for what the future held for us. God knew that I needed to be complete and He was not going to forsake me. I can see the pain and suffering I experiences through these trials has brought me closer to God and showed me how to live an abundant life that is fully submitted to Him. C.S. Lewis stated it so well when he said this:

> "God loves us, so He makes us the gift of suffering. Through suffering, we release our hold on the toys of this world, and know our true good lies in another world.

> We're like blocks of stone, out of which the sculptor carves the forms of men. The blows of his chisel, which hurt us so much, are what make us perfect. The suffering in this world is not the failure of God's love for us; it is that love in action. For believe me, this world that seems to us so substantial is no more than the shadowlands. Real life has not begun yet."

Without the suffering that I was enduring, and the heartache that I was going through, I would not know to release those things of the world in expectation for better things, for things not of this world. I would not see God's love for me! I needed to see God's love so that I could fully love Him. God is more focused on our eternal lives than our momentary comforts. We will live eternity either in Heaven with our Father, or forever apart from Him and His goodness in Hell. God loves us and wants us to live eternally with Him, so our momentary suffering and our trials are preparing us and refining us to live holy lives and to live an eternal life with our Lord. He wants us to live victoriously in this life as well so that through our triumphs and victories, we can help others overcome. Through our stories of God's love and redemption, we can share hope in our Lord. Revelations 12:11 says "and they overcame him (the devil) by the blood of the Lamb and by the word of their testimony". Our story, our triumph over trials and tribulations, and God's power through it all is what will help us overcome Satan. Our testimonies are what gives others the strength to also overcome. God cares about each and every person's eternal life. He cares so much that He sent His only Son to born as a human on earth, persecuted, beaten, whipped, humiliated, and killed on a cross. All to save us from the eternal torment in Hell that we deserve for our sins. "For everyone has sinned; we all fall short of God's glorious standard. Yet God, in his grace, freely makes us right in his sight. He did this through Christ Jesus when he freed us from the penalty for our sins. For God presented Jesus as the sacrifice for sin. People are made right with God when they believe that Jesus sacrificed his life, shedding his blood. This sacrifice shows that God was being fair when he held back and did not punish those who sinned in times past." Romans 3:23-25. The most precious sacrifice was made for us. My sins, my trials, my torment, and my suffering was helping me to release the hold on worldly things so that I could fully grasp onto the most precious sacrifice that is Jesus Christ.

I contemplated leaving Stetson, taking Lynlee and going back home to my parent's house. Shame and fear kept me from it. I could not bear to look into my parents' sad and disappointed eyes every day. I was afraid of what Stetson would do to himself if I left. While Stetson was reckless with his own life, he loved me, and he loved Lynlee. He didn't want us to go, but he was so swept up in this hurricane Satan had him in. He could see the pain and destruction, but he was helpless to do anything about it. Satan had lied to him, telling him there was no way out of the pain. So, the hurricane raged on. He was doing meth constantly. He would be gone for days and come home in a fit of rage and paranoia. The pattern would repeat. I went to work, took care of Lynlee, and survived. The fog kept me from looking towards the future or asking Stetson what he was doing. I did not know or understand that his days were filled with drugs and despair. I was hidden from the ugly truth that Stetson was addicted to meth. My island kept me from others so no one else asked what was going on. I was alone in my grief and despair. Stetson's parents tried to help, but they were at a loss about what to do. How can you help someone who doesn't want help? How can you help someone who has hurt you, used you, and abused you at every turn? I know now, that their prayers for Stetson and I are what changed everything. My mother's prayers helped change everything. The people around us praying helped change everything. Dear friend, if you know someone that is in a pit, pray for them without ceasing. The outcome may look grim, you may not see any change, but I promise that God is faithful. He hears your prayers; he hears your cries for help. He sees people's pain and he longs to heal it. 1 John 5:14 says "and we are confident that he hears us whenever we ask for anything that pleases him." We can be confident that He hears our prayers and is He is faithful to answer. The prayers of desperation that people were praying for us were preparing to be answered.

A change came one day, almost two years after Lynlee was born. For almost two years we had been digging ourselves into a pit, living this life of chaos and confusion. While I was at work, Stetson's dad came in and said he was taking Stetson to rehab. He said that Stetson was into something bad at our house, and he was worse that he had ever seen him. My stomach dropped and my heart stopped. I had no clue that Stetson was that far into drugs. In my mind I thought, "He has to be mistaken! Stetson doesn't do drugs!" Our chaos of each day had become normal, so I could not see how serious and damaged we both were. At the time, I thought I was naïve and stupid for not seeing it, for not seeing the drugs in Stetson's life. I knew he was a different person than when I met him, but I never really thought about why he changed. Satan was blinding me from the truth. Satan was blinding me from what he was doing in our lives so I would not question anything. Satan put fog around my island to blind, confuse, and isolate me. But my God is stronger than the enemy. God used every weapon that Satan was using against me, for my good. He was still using the fog to protect me and keep me where I needed to be, and He kept me there with Stetson for a reason. God placed me in this painful place so that I could feel the joy and abounding love that I feel now. I was emotionally and mentally abused and exhausted every day for two years, but it was not in vain. Had I not gone through that, I would not be as strong as I am today. "'When you go through deep waters, I will be with you. When you go through rivers of difficulty, you will not drown. When you walk through the fire of oppression, you will not be burned up; the flames will not consume you.'" Isaiah 43:2. The flames were not consuming me, though it may have felt like it. They were refining me and strengthening me. Satan thought he was destroying me, but my God does not let His precious children be destroyed. I may have felt lost, but God saw me and knew where I was. God knew what my future held, and he was allowing the fire to renew me for the future. 1 Peter 5:10 says "In his kindness God called you to share in his eternal glory by means of Christ Jesus. So after you have suffered a little while, he will restore, support, and strengthen you, and he will place you on a firm foundation." All things that I needed! I needed to be restored from the aimless person I was. I needed support and strength for my family's future, and I needed a firm foundation to build my life and my family's life on. I could not gain these things without my suffering. While God was shielding me, he was also preparing to restore me.

Brandon and I loaded up Stetson, slightly willingly, and took him to rehab. Then began the worst two hours of my life, and I had thought it couldn't get any worse. Stetson was a new level of high that day. He was angrier and more disrespectful than I had ever seen him. Imagine a rabid, angry badger locked in a little cage. He seemed less willing the further we drove. He tried to kick out the windows. He dumped bottles of water all over me and the pickup. We had to stop when we were almost there and Stetson got out and just walked off. I wasn't sure if he was going to come back. But he did, and we kept going. I can see now, that this was Satan's attempt to derail us from where God was taking us because rehab was the first step in healing for Stetson. When you are on the road to redemption, Satan will throw anything he can at you to derail and discourage you. He will do anything to keep you from having what God has in store for you. When God is moving and working in your life, Satan will try to destroy it. The Heavenly Father cannot be defeated though, because He has already won the war that day on Calvary. The day that Jesus hung and died on the cross, to bear our sins and burdens, was the day that Satan was defeated forever and ever. God is victorious, and through Jesus Christ, we are also victorious. He was not going to allow Satan to win this fight, and neither were we.

We were taking Stetson to rehab if it killed us. God was giving us the strength to survive. Whether it worked or not, at least we would get a week of peace, I thought.

Stetson got checked in for rehab, and I went home. I was home alone with Lynlee, and I felt some semblance of peace for the first time in two years. I did not have to worry about Stetson barging in and yelling at me about who knows what. I didn't have to worry about Stetson calling me and being paranoid about where I was. I wanted rehab to help but I was not hopeful. Hope felt like a distant memory. I couldn't remember the last time I felt hope. I had become afraid to hope because I had not felt joy or peace in so long. The hope that God once showed me had dissipated at the next lie Satan told me. Satan is a thief and he was stealing my hope. Friend, there is always hope. Hope in God and his unfailing love. Romans 15:13 sums it up quite well. "I pray that God, the source of hope, will fill you completely with joy and peace because you trust in him. Then you will overflow with confident hope through the power of the Holy Spirit." God is our source of hope. Our hope in Him fills us and overflows. Do not let Satan steal your precious hope. He can only steal what we *allow* him to steal. I was allowing him to steal everything from me. I was not putting up a fight, I was not letting God fight for me. I had rolled over and allowed Satan to run rampant in my life and take it over. But God is on my side and He was fighting for me. God came to my defense because He loved me. God was going to give me hope, and He was going to grow it until it was overflowing. God is our source of hope and through trusting in Him, we can overflow with confident hope.

While Stetson was at rehab, I took Lynlee to visit my

parents. I had just found out I was pregnant again, and I was even more lost. Becoming pregnant again felt like another stumbling block, pushing my island of isolation further away. I had been on my island of isolation so long and I couldn't see through the fog. This pregnancy felt like more shame being heaped on me when I already was bent so low. The visit with my parents was awkward and sad. They asked me where Stetson was, and I could not lie. I told them he was in rehab, but I could not make myself tell them it was for meth. They tried to help me and ask me to come live with them. My mom could tell I was pregnant. I could see the sadness they had for me, and they wanted me to be ok. Then we had a conversation that I will never forget. My dad said that Stetson will never change and that I need to leave. My heart broke. I knew deep down he was right, but I also knew that I couldn't leave him alone. As much as I was hurting, I could see that he was also hurting. It hurt me every day to see this boy that I fell in love with, that was so full of life, so defeated and angry all the time. As much as I hurt, I still wanted to be there for him. My mom then said that yes, he can change but *only God can help him*. She still had faith. She still knew that God is a miracle worker and could transform any life. She was clinging on to God's truth. In Mark 11:24, Jesus states, "I tell you, you can pray for anything, and if you believe that you've received it, it will be yours." She was confident in Jesus' words! She was standing on her foundation of Jesus Christ, declaring that God can change Stetson. She was standing in the gap for us, believing that God could change our lives. I did not believe her at this point. I had been so defeated and beat down that I couldn't let myself believe that. I hadn't seen God work in my life that significantly so I didn't think it could happen. Little did I know what all God had been doing in my life the whole time. I couldn't see it, but it was more than I could ever have imagined. God was preparing to show me how miraculous He could work.

Stetson called me four days into his weeklong stint at rehab saying he was checking himself out. He said he was better. I highly doubted that, but I went to get him anyway. I was so jaded and bitter from all the hurt I had experienced; I couldn't imagine him being better or changing. I brought him home, and he started to try and explain some things to me. He explained the hold that drugs had over his life. He explained how he always desired to stay home and spend time with us, but something stronger than him was always pulling him away. The drugs had a hold over his life that he was unable to control. Now, after having my mind opened, I can see how Satan used the drugs as a trap. Once Stetson began using drugs, Satan trapped him in a hurricane. Satan intended to strand Stetson in this hurricane just like he intended to strand me on my island. Stetson was reaching out, trying to show me what the drugs were doing to him. The drugs were taking away his choices. He stated that he was going to try to change. Rehab had showed him that he didn't have to rely on drugs. He tried to stay clean for a few days and got a job. However, after a few days, the pull of drugs that Satan put in his life could not be defeated alone. Stetson was using drugs to fill a hole in his life and removing the drugs left an even bigger hole. This hole is where God should have been in his life. Trying to stuff worldly things in our life where God should be will leave us emptier than when we started. Rehab started his journey of trying to stay clean, but he could not do it by himself. The more he would try, the more frustrated he would become when he fell short. He quit his job because the pull of drugs was too strong. He quickly fell back into his old habits of doing drugs. Stetson could not change his life on his own, without God's help. He saw in rehab that he did not have to rely on drugs, but he could not see what else to rely on. He did not realize yet that his reliance should be on our Holy Creator. We could not have a victorious life without God's help. Philippians 2:13 says, "For God is working in you, giving you the desire and the power to do what pleases him." We could not please Him, and we could not change ourselves without God's help and without Him giving us a desire to please Him. We did not know or understand this. We were not yet living to please God. Yes, we knew about God, but we had been listening and following Satan for so long God's voice of truth was far away from us. Had we asked Him to help, had we asked Him to show us how to please Him, He would have been right there for us. Thankfully, that day finally came.

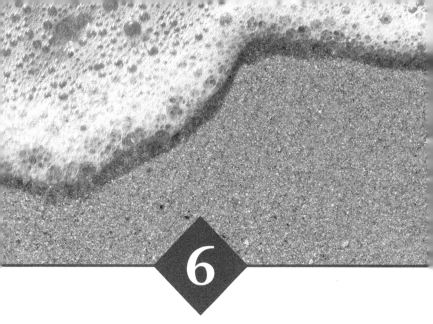

The Rescue

"For he has rescued us from the kingdom
of darkness and transferred us into the
Kingdom of his dear Son, who purchased
our freedom and forgave our sins."

Colossians 1:13-14

We were in the midst of a heated, late-night argument about the same old ridiculous things. Chaos, anger, and confusion were running rampant. The argument made its way outside where Stetson was trying to leave and I was begging him not to. I was always so afraid of what would happen to him when he would leave, always afraid it might be the last time I would see him. We were both at each other's throats, yelling and screaming. Stetson shouted, and fell to his knees, becoming quiet. He sat there a moment. He stood up and looked around. I angrily said, "What's the matter with you?" Stetson calmly replied "I don't know, but something is different. I feel something I have never felt before." Today, this is one of my favorite things to hear Stetson talk about. The first time he felt the peace of God. When he fell to his knees, he prayed "Lord, I need you." He meant it with every fiber of his being. This prayer came from the depths of his tormented soul. He was tired of living this way and wanted to change. He was tired of seeing destruction and heartache everywhere. He had realized he could not do it on his own. God answered immediately because He had always been right there, waiting for that moment. "Then I called on the name of the Lord: 'Please, Lord, save me!' How kind the Lord is! How good He is! So merciful, this God of ours!" Psalms 116:4-5. Stetson says now that as soon as he prayed that prayer, he felt something leave him, like a cover being pulled off a car. He felt the hurt, anger, and confusion leave him. He felt peace inside of him. Not a mellowed-out peace from drugs, but an all-consuming, life-changing peace. The peace of God. Me, being so weathered and worn down from the hurt and anger, basically said whatever and went inside. I didn't know what was going on. I assumed he had finally gone full crazy. I had become so bitter from not feeling and shutting off my emotions and thoughts. I was so bitter towards him and everything around me that I couldn't imagine him or anything changing. But after that night, he did.

A wise man once showed me a quote by James Stewart,

a minister in the early 1900's, which rings true for this situation. It is as follows:

> "It is a glorious phrase of the New Testament, that 'he led captivity captive.' The very triumphs of His foes, it means, he used for their defeat. He compelled their dark achievements to sub-serve his end, not theirs. They nailed him to the tree, not knowing that by that very act they were bringing the world to his feet. They gave him a cross, not guessing that he would make it a throne. They flung him outside the gates to die, not knowing that in that very moment they were lifting up all the gates of the universe, to let the King of Glory come in. They thought to root out his doctrines, not understanding that they were implanting imperishably in the hearts of men the very name they intended to destroy. They thought they had defeated God with His back the wall, pinned and helpless and defeated: they did not know that it was God Himself who had tracked them down. He did not conquer in spite of the dark mystery of evil. He conquered through it."

Satan thought he was destroying Stetson with the drugs, the lies, and the deceit. He didn't know how great my God is. God triumphed *through* the darkness. He *used* the darkness that Satan had created to break through to Stetson by taking it away, by showing his peace and love that Stetson had never experienced before. Satan brought Stetson into the darkness not knowing that the King of Glory would burst through and save his child. Satan brought Stetson to the deepest pit, not knowing that God was waiting for him there. God used this pit to raise him up. "He did not conquer in spite of the dark mystery of evil. He conquered through it." God used this moment, bursting through the darkness, to begin to change Stetson. He tore the veil of darkness and let the light in. And by changing Stetson, He began the process of changing me.

It was not an immediate change. It was slow and laborious. Stetson felt God beginning to fill the hole in his life. That hole that Satan told Stetson could only be fixed with drugs, was being filled with the Holy One who created that hole. God created us with a desire for Him, and only He can fill it. Stetson was being filled with his Creator, so the desire to do drugs waned. The fights and arguments were still constant, but he began to slowly come home more and do drugs less. God was giving Stetson a new desire, but his mind was still clouded with the confusion, hate, and lies that Satan and the drugs instilled in him. He got a job building fence and worked so hard at it. He worked for a wonderful man who expected a lot out of him and would hold him accountable. Due to Stetsons DUI's, he couldn't drive, so his mom or I had to take him to and from work. It was a struggle and exhausting, but Stetson was trying. He wanted to go to work and provide for us. He wanted to be there for his family. We began going to little church with his parents. I was still bitter and angry, but if Stetson wanted to go to church and try to get better, then I would go with him. In the beginning, I wasn't going to hear God or to love on Him. I was just going to make sure Stetson was going so that he could get better. Whatever reason that you are in church though, God will break through. God was and still is filling that church, and his goodness was all around us. Every Sunday we went, was another day that we heard God's word, another day that brought us closer to our day of redemption. I may have been there for the wrong reason, but God was not going to let Satan win while I was sitting in His House. While I was sitting in church, hoping that it was helping Stetson, God was helping me. In that church, God was thinning my fog. God was opening my eyes and helping me to see clearly. God was removing the confusion and the naivety. I could see the reason Stetson was acting the way that he was. I could see where his paranoia and anger were stemming from. I began to see that drugs had invaded Stetsons mind and changed him. I began to be able to see how the drugs were affecting him physically and emotionally. Little by little, he was doing drugs less. I knew the reasons behind his actions now, so I kept watch. I became angry and paranoid. I was monitoring every action, word, and movement that Stetson made, trying to determine if he was of sound mind. On days he didn't do drugs, he was slightly calmer.

I began to question him to ensure that he was not doing drugs. I was trying to control the situation and make Stetson do the right thing. I would ask him questions that made it seem like I wanted to know what he did that day, but I just wanted to make sure he didn't do drugs. I inspected his face and actions to ensure he hadn't done drugs. I kept count of the days he was sober. I read in one of his rehab books that if a drug addict can stay clean for 90 days, then they are more likely to stay clean. I was obsessed with marking days, counting down until 90 days, but I would become so disappointed when I could tell he did drugs. Every time I had to start the 90 days over felt like a punch in the gut. I tried to guilt him and make him feel bad for doing it. I went from having no control, to trying to control everything. But I was only human. Nothing I could have done or anything I did do is what made Stetson change. I was beating my head against a wall trying to fix him, but luckily, it was not up to me to fix Stetson. We as humans can do nothing without God. Jesus tells us in John 15:5, "'Yes, I am the vine; you are the branches. Those who remain in me, and I in them, will produce much fruit. For apart from me you can do nothing.'" I could not have made Stetson change, no matter how bad I wanted to. All my railroading, all my cajoling was in vain. I was apart from God, so I could not do anything to help. In John 6:63, Jesus says, "'The Spirit alone gives eternal life. Human effort accomplishes nothing.'" My meager efforts were no good. Jesus said the Spirit is what gives life. I am so glad that it was not up to me to change Stetson because my human brain could not have fathomed how much God planned to change Stetson. God was planning a miraculous renewal in Stetson and myself that no human, no mere mortal, could have invented or accomplished. "'My thoughts are nothing like your thoughts,' says the Lord. 'And my ways are far beyond anything you could imagine. For just as the heavens are higher than the earth, so my ways are higher than your ways and my thoughts higher than your thoughts.'" Isiah 55:8-9. We cannot imagine the good things God has in store for us because we do not think like Him.

Just like we cannot try to do anything apart from Him, we cannot put God in a box. We cannot limit Him to what we *think* He can do. God can "accomplish infinitely more than we might ask or think." Ephesians 3:20. I could not imagine the miraculous things that were coming, so I was doing what I knew to do. I was in survival mode. I was trying to not be a victim anymore. I was not going to let drugs ruin our lives anymore. God was helping me see, but he was also preparing me for what lay ahead. Thankfully, there were powers much more powerful than me at work in our lives.

We still would argue and fight, and Stetson was still paranoid, but we were improving, little by little. He began talking to me about God and how he wants to change. I just listened and nodded, still feeling isolated, but wanting Stetson to be better. If this is what was going to make him change and be better, then I would listen and attend church with him. I was just going with the flow, still surviving. Every time that he would slip up and do drugs again, I would be so frustrated wondering why this wasn't working, why he couldn't stop. Every time though, Stetson would show remorse, something that had never happened before. Our fights began to change into Stetson pouring out his thoughts about God. He would talk for hours and hours while I listened. Stetson was telling me things that God had been showing him and how much love God had for him. I could see something different inside of Stetson, but it was different and unknown, so I was afraid. I was afraid of what could come from change. Satan was still instilling fear into me, making sure I would not reach out from my island of isolation. I was afraid to hope that my life could get better, but God kept moving in our lives, freeing me from this fear bit by bit.

Stetson told our preacher one day that he wanted to get baptized. I was glad and hoped that he would go through with it, hoping it would make him better. Stetson didn't come home the night before he was to get baptized. He did not come home until very early in the morning, and I could tell that he was high. I was so angry and disappointed. I could not believe that he would do that to me, to his parents, and to the preacher. I was more worried about what people would think and how this affected me than anything else. I never stopped to think why Stetson wanted to get baptized. I never stopped to think if this meant that Stetson was actually being changed by God. I just thought this was a step in his recovery. I was still so blinded by the fog. I may have been able to see Stetson's faults more clearly, but I was not seeing God clearly. Satan was still blinding me to God's love and goodness. I was looking at Stetson's recovery through worldly eyes. I just wanted him to get *better*. I just wanted a change. I wasn't wanting a life renewal or a redemption, so I wasn't seeking that. I was just looking for *better*. Just better is not what God wanted for my life. God wanted to radically change, transform, and renew my life. All because he loved me. He wasn't going to settle for either one of our lives being *only* better. God loved me enough to keep pushing until we were both renewed, redeemed, and reclaimed as Children of God.

I can now see this as one of Satan's ploys to keep Stetson from this blessing. Satan was once again trying to do everything in his power to keep us from moving forward in our walk and our journey to God's love. I was too stubborn and angry to not let Stetson do it. I told him that he needs to suck it up and do it because he said he would. Not because it's what God wanted for his life, and not because this is another step towards Jesus and recovery. I was so lost and confused that I couldn't even see the blessing that this was going to be. I just wanted Stetson to go through with it so that people wouldn't ask questions or be disappointed. I was still so filled with shame; I couldn't stand the thought of letting people down. So, at my misguided urging, Stetson got baptized. He bravely went forward in front of the church, and our preacher submerged him. He became washed clean from the sins of his past. He was declaring in front of everyone that Jesus Christ was his Savior and he chose to follow him. 1 Peter 3:21 states, "And that water is a picture of baptism, which now saves you, not by removing dirt from your body, but as a response to God from a clean conscience. It is effective because of the resurrection of Jesus Christ." The baptism was not effective because I forced him to do it. It was effective because God is good. God wanted Stetson to be cleansed by Jesus' blood, to have a clear conscience so he could begin living in the freedom that was bought with Jesus' blood. God desired to wipe away all the confusions, hate, anger, lies, fear, and shame that Satan had put into Stetson's heart and mind. Jesus paid the price for every person's freedom and God desired Stetson to live in that freedom. God had a plan for Stetson's life and nothing on this earth, nothing that Satan could do to him, could derail what God had set in motion. God himself tells us in Isaiah 14:27, "'The Lord of Heavens' Armies has spoken-who can change his plans? When his hand is raised, who can stop him?'" God's plan cannot be stopped or changed.

He desired to change Stetson's life, to change my life, so His plan was prevailing. Stetson began to rely more on God and His love. He started to live in the freedom that Jesus bought for him, and he began to allow Jesus to transform his life.

I began to see a shift in Stetson's life. I began to notice that he was not as angry and paranoid. He would sit at the kitchen table, absorbed in his Bible. I was still on my island of isolation, so I couldn't reach out and ask him to help me see what he was seeing in God. I was so used to taking care of myself, and so filled with shame and anxiety, I couldn't ask for help. I saw him changing, and was so glad for it. I did not realize I could or needed to change as well. I was getting what I wanted, Stetson to be better. I would have been complacent with that, but God was not complacent. God wanted all of me. God did not desire only Stetson to be freed, but me as well. He loved me with an all-consuming love that spans time. God began my healing and freedom through Stetson's resurrection.

He began to apologize to me for all the wrong he had done, and for leaving me and Lynlee alone. I told him I forgave him. And I did. There was no part of me that held anything against Stetson. Forgiving him was the easiest thing I had ever done because I wanted to forgive him. This was what I had wanted all along, for him to be better. I wanted to leave everything in the past and forget it. I wanted us to be *better* so how could I keep us from that? I couldn't hold a grudge against him and make things harder, so I forgave him. I wanted to move on with our lives and be happy. Stetson could not understand how I could forgive him just like that. He could not understand how I was not angry and upset with him for everything he had done. I can see now that this is where my healing began. This is where the fog began to dissipate, and the island began to crumble. Extending forgiveness began to heal me and open my eyes. I did not quite understand how I so easily forgave Stetson either. Until God began to show me. Jesus says in Matthew 6:14-15 that "'If you forgive those who sin against you, your heavenly Father will forgive you. But if you refuse to forgive others, your Father will not forgive your sins.'" God was handing me forgiveness while I was giving Stetson forgiveness. God knew we needed to heal and be forgiven, so He put forgiveness in my heart to heal both of us. He wanted our sins washed away and forgiven so that we could live lives of victory. My sins needed to be forgiven just like Stetson's did. We could not live free with the shackles of our past sins and we could not move forward into God's presence with unforgiveness in our hearts. I needed to be forgiven so that I could cast off my shame and condemnation. So, God put forgiveness in our hearts. God gave us what we needed to live free lives.

We continued to go to church, I kept hearing the Word of God, and the church members and the preacher kept loving on us. They did not treat us differently, and they did not shun us. I knew they could have, two aimless souls, not married, already with a child and one on the way. They never judged us, only loved us. I saw the love they had for us and knew that this was not an earthly love. I could see that this was the love that God had for his people. I began to see that the forgiveness that I had given Stetson, was the forgiveness that God had for us. I knew that I could not have forgiven him so easily. God was clearing the fog and showing me that He was helping me forgive Stetson so that

I could live in freedom, and so that I could have a better and victorious life as well. God did not want to hold his past against him, just like he did not want me to be stranded on that island. He did not want my sins to hold me back. He did not want shame to hold me captive any longer. God keeps no record of wrongs nor holds your past against you. It has been washed away by the blood of Jesus. When Jesus died on the cross, he died carrying all our sins, our past, our brokenness, and our shame. Hebrews 10:10 says "for God's will was for us to be made holy by the sacrifice of the body of Jesus Christ, *once for all time.*" God had a will for our lives, and it was not to live the life Satan was pushing us towards. He wanted us to live holy through Jesus Christ. God was removing my fog to see His love clearly. He was miraculously changing Stetson so that he could love and be loved. God used him and how He was changing him, to change me. He used the forgiveness I extended, to help Stetson and myself be set free.

One day we were talking, and we decided to set a date to get married before we had our second child. This was a big and monumental step for me. I had never before considered actually marrying Stetson. Yes, we had rings, and yes, we were technically engaged, but I could not have imagined marrying him the way he used to be. Before, I never considered actually marrying him because I did not want to have to think about divorce. I did not want to think about being shackled to the sad life I was leading, but that life was disappearing. God was moving in our lives, changing us and renewing us. I could see that I would have a happy life with Stetson. I could see peace in him. I did not see the happy boy I once knew, but a joy-filled man of

God. We were not perfect, and we still fought at times, but I could see God shining through him and the Holy Spirit working in him. He was slowly being changed by God's love. I began to see Stetson choosing me, choosing to spend time with me. I was aware that the island of isolation was crumbling. I wanted him in my life, I wanted his company and his joy filled spirit in my life. I wanted to leave my island that Satan had told me I belonged on. God was beginning to show me that I was not created to be alone. God created Stetson and I to be together, to be there for each other, to build each other up, and to grow in God together. God was restoring us both and restoring our relationship. We began to trust each other as God healed us. We had to work to trust each other, though. We had to rely on God, and we had to let go of our past hurts. We had to *choose* to let go of the hurt and anger inside of us, with God's help. He was showing us the Truth that set us free. He showed us that Jesus came to give us a life filled with the loving fruits of the Spirit, not evil spirits that torment. Jesus came to heal us of our past transgressions and remove our past of hurt and despair. I could see God bringing us together. I was excited and ready to marry Stetson. I was ready to live a life of peace and love. I was ready to leave behind my sinful ways and acknowledge God.

We got married on August 11. We began our new life together. It felt like a new and fresh start. We made a covenant in front of God to love each other no matter what. We were committed to each other. Our wonderful preacher read Ecclesiastes 4:12, and this is when I began to realize that God was molding us to become a triple-braided cord, relying on Him. I saw clearly that Stetson and I had to become one unit, relying on God. My fog of confusion was gone. I saw clearly the love that God had for me, for my family that I thought was so shameful. I saw that God had chosen to love us. I saw that Stetson, Lynlee, and I were always loved and cared for. I asked the preacher to read Ruth 1:16. "Ruth replied, 'Don't ask me to leave you and turn back. Wherever you go, I will go; wherever you live, I will live. Your people will be my people, and your God will be my God." I wanted Stetson to know that I would never leave him. I wanted him to know that no matter what we had been through, or what the future held, I loved him fiercely. I was ready to leave my island of isolation and join him. I was ready to rely on God and build our life together on more than just an island. We had been through torment and anguish together and came out on the other side stronger. All because of our great God. God saw us through, and He brought us back together. He showed me that I could live off of my island of isolation, so He removed me from the island that Satan trapped me on and intended to strand me on, forever alone. God showed me that I do not have to be isolated, that I do not have to close myself off to people. He showed me that I can have a foundation of trust, love, and grace. Not through a human, and not through anything the world can offer me. It is only through Jesus Christ who died to set me free. He used the island to free me. When God first created the world in Genesis 2:18, He stated, "It is not good for the man to be alone." God saw that we cannot live and flourish alone, He saw that we need people around us to love and care for. He saw that we need other people to thrive and that we are stronger together. God used the island to show me that I can love, and be free. Free from isolation.

Free to love people and rely on them. Free to rely on Him and trust in His love for us. I was no longer alone and afraid. God's face was shining on me, Stetson, and our precious children. Our second child, Madison Faye, was born a few months later. A miraculous gift from God. God knew what he was doing when he placed these sweet little girls in our life. They are blessings from God that we do not deserve, but He graciously placed them with us. His grace and mercy was, and still is, abounding in our family. "Instead of shame and dishonor, you will enjoy a double share of honor. You will possess a double portion of prosperity in your land, and everlasting joy will be yours." Isaiah 61:7. God was fulfilling this promise in our lives. He was bringing us into miraculous blessings that He had laid out for us.

Our healing and renewal were not an instant thing. It was a gradual healing that required us to rely on God's love. There were still times that shame gripped me and told me that I did not deserve what I had been given. There were times that anger still took hold of Stetson. I still struggled with the desire to control everything and everyone around me. The past hurt and anger tripped us up at times, and at times we tried to throw the past in each other's faces. But we did not let this define us. We had grown and realized that this was Satan trying to trip us up. Our spiritual eyes were open and we could now see Satan trying to destroy us with these feelings and emotions. We clung onto God and his promises for us. We pushed through the hard times and the attacks of Satan. We desired to be completely free. I began listening to God's voice and relying on His Love for me. God was healing my mind and heart. He was removing the lies that Satan had instilled in us. He was doing a movement in our lives so big and miraculous, that when I look back on it, I am flooded with love. God loved us at our worst, when we had no love for Him. He took care of us in the darkness when we were not even seeking the light. He saved us and changed us when the world said we could not be saved or changed. "And I am convinced that nothing can ever separate us from God's love. Neither death nor life, neither angels nor demons, neither our fears for today nor our worries about tomorrow- not even the powers of hell can separate us from God's love. No power in the sky about or in the earth below- indeed nothing in all creation will ever be able to separate us from the love of God that is revealed in Christ Jesus our Lord." Romans 8:38-39. Nothing we did, nothing Satan did, nothing the world said, ever separated us from God's love.

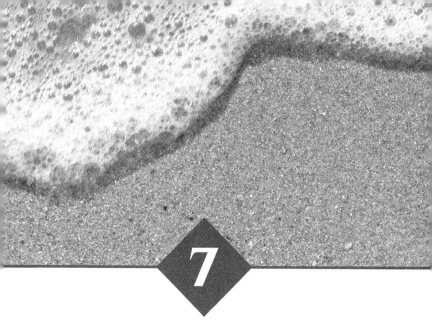

The Mountain

"For every child of God defeats this evil world, and we achieve this victory through our faith. And who can win this battle against the world? Only those who believe that Jesus is the Son of God."

1 John 5:4-5

Stetson and I's past is not something I ever want to forget. I want to always remember the pit that we were in because I want to remember that *God met us in the pit.* God did not forsake us, He did not turn his back on us, even when we dug the pit ourselves. Even when we wallowed in our pit, allowing Satan to run rampant in our lives, God did not forsake us. God says in Hebrews 13:5 "Never will I leave you; never will I forsake you." This is a promise from God that cannot be revoked. This promise cannot be affected or ruled null. Not even if we turn our backs on God. Not even if Satan has us in his clutches. Not even if we feel like there is no hope. Not even if we feel like we are in the deepest, darkest pit. *God will never leave or forsake you.*

While I will never forget the past, I do not dwell on it. I dwell on God's love, grace, and mercy. I look at my family and praise God for where he has brought us. My soul rejoices for the joy that He has given me. My soul was once tormented, bitter, isolated, and deep in the darkest pit of Satan's hate. God rescued my soul, bringing it into the light. Where I once experienced darkness and evil, I now live in the Light and God's goodness. Such darkness makes the light even brighter. Such hate and torment makes the love and peace I feel so much more fulfilling. The peace of God is now sacred to me. My soul is filled with praise for my mighty Lord and Savior. "I love the Lord because he hears my voice and my prayer for mercy. Because he bends down to listen, I will pray as long as I have breath!" Psalms 116:1-2. I will praise God every day for who He is because of the darkness I have felt and experienced. I will praise Him not just because He has been good *to* me, but also because He *is* good. God is the very definition of good, no matter what our circumstances are. Jesus himself tells the people in Mark 10:18, "Only God is truly good." He *is* goodness. God also tells us who He is in Exodus 34:6. He tells Moses, "Yahweh! The Lord! The God of compassion and mercy! I am slow to anger and filled with unfailing love and faithfulness." These are not just descriptions of

God, but *who* God is. God is the very root of goodness, compassion, mercy, and love. Without God, we cannot have those things, and without those things is darkness. But God sent His Son Jesus so that we may also have these things! "The Word gave life to everything that was created, and his life brought light to everyone. The light shines in the darkness, and the darkness can never extinguish it." John 1:4-5. Jesus gives us the attributes of God so that we may be light in this dark world. God's light shines in us so that we may chase away the darkness of this world and be God's light. My soul is filled with the glorious Light of my Lord, a light that can never be extinguished, so I will forever praise my Lord and Savior. "For once you were full of darkness, but now you have light from the Lord. So live as people of light! For this light within you produces only what is good and right and true." Ephesians 5:8-9.

God has touched not only me and Stetson, but those around us as well. God gave us the Light so those around us could see the Light and be changed by the Light just like we were. God has restored the relationship between my parents and I. God brought my dad closer to Him. He goes to church every Sunday and tells me he is praying for me. They live right down the road from us and it brings my heart joy to go see them without fear of shame and condemnation. God has restored the relationship between Stetson and his parents. Stetson loves to talk to his parents and discuss anything you can think of. He has no fear of feeling shame from them anymore. They love him with an everlasting love. God has restored my relationships with my friends. We love to go to Christian conferences and praise God together. One of my best friends is now my neighbor, and we get to glorify

God together as strong women of faith. I am so thankful for this friend that God has brought back into my life. God has restored my relationship with people. I no longer fear condemnation from others. I no longer feel isolated from others. Satan still tries to grip me with fear, telling me that I am not worthy to reach out to others. But now that my spiritual eyes have been opened, I can see the lies. I can see that God created me to share His love. God has given me a love for people. God has given us two beautiful, smart, loving, kind and God-loving girls. I look into their beautiful faces and know that I did nothing to deserve such perfect children. I look at my life with my husband and know that I did nothing to deserve how happy we are together. God restored and renewed our relationship to be a relationship that is built on Jesus. God has poured and overflowed his love, grace, truth, and mercy onto us. God does not hold my past against me, He does not condemn me for not living the way I should have, or for not seeking him daily. He does not condemn me for listening to the lies of Satan. Romans 8:1-2 says "So now there is no condemnation for those who belong to Christ Jesus. And because you belong to him, the power of the life-giving Spirit has freed you from the power of sin that leads to death." I belong to God, and He has freed me from the power that sin had over my life. God has freed me from living a life of despair, to living the life that He has prepared for me. He is forming me and making me look like Him. God removed my shame and guilt. He showed me that I am *chosen* by Him. " …for you are a chosen people. You are royal priests, a holy nation, God's very own possession. As a result, you can show others the goodness of God, for he called you out of the darkness into his wonderful light."

1 Peter 2:9. He showed me what my true name was. Not the names that Satan tried to convince me that I was: hopeless, alone, ruined, shameful. God cleansed me from the filth that Satan put on me, from the ashes that my life was in. He clothed me in purity and freedom. He showed me who I truly am in Him: pure, chosen, holy, fulfilled, loved. He saved me from the pit, removed me from my island, and raised me from the ashes, so my lips will forever praise Him.

God's grace and mercy has brought us to a place filled with joy, peace, and love. We have continued to go to our small hometown church, and we have thrived there. The church members have accepted us, supported us, and loved us. After a few years, Stetson was asked to become the youth leader. I could not have been prouder or more filled with love. God raised Stetson up from a drug addict to a youth minister who shows the children God's love every Wednesday. God has blessed our youth group beyond anything I could have imagined. More and more kids began coming, and we soon had a very large group attending. There were all different age groups, so I began teaching the younger children on Wednesday nights as well. We love these Wednesday nights that we get to share God's love with His precious children. God raised me up from a pregnant teen who knew nothing about how to raise children, to a lover of children. God was leading me down a road to find my purpose. I had spent years wandering, not knowing what my calling was, and not knowing what to do with my life. God knew all along and he was preparing me for my future. God created me with a purpose, and he helped me to find it. He led me to a job working with children in a school. This is where I discovered my God-given purpose to become a teacher. I fought it for a while, not knowing if I was worthy to teach. I did not feel worthy to teach with the past that I had. Shame was trying to grip me again. I did not feel that I had enough love, patience, and grace inside of me to help children. I did not have those things, but God did. By myself I was not worthy, but God made me worthy. My past sins said that I was not worthy to be the kind of teacher that children need. But my past was nailed to the cross and Jesus made me worthy. 2 Thessalonians 1:11-12 says "So we keep on praying for you, asking our God to enable you to live a life worthy of his call. May he give you the power to accomplish all the good things your faith prompts you to do. Then the name of our Lord Jesus will be honored because of the way you live, and you will be honored along with him. This is all made possible because of the grace of our God and Lord, Jesus Christ." Jesus made me worthy through his sacrifice so that I could bring glory and honor to the Father. That is my purpose in life, to live each day for His Glory. God was showing me what my purpose was so that I could honor Him and share in His honor.

God delivered me from an island of isolation to His Mountain of Glory. He restored and renewed me. All because He loves me. Not because of whose child I am, not because of where I'm from, and not because of who my friends are. It is all because I am a unique creation of God and He loves me. "God saved you by his grace when you believed. And you can't take credit for this; it is a gift from God." Ephesians 2:8. I was saved by the grace of God. He restored and renewed Stetson. His mind was filled with anger, paranoia, hate, and lies from Satan. God has cleared His mind, filled him with the Holy Spirit, and taken away his pain from the past. God did not only save him from the drugs, but He also renewed his mind from the effects of the drugs. His mind is clear and filled with God's Word. Stetson asked God to take away the memories of torment and anguish that Satan caused him. God heard him and answered him. He doesn't remember the darkest times and most of his tormented time on drugs, because God heard his prayer for mercy and lifted his head. God renewed his mind and gave him a zeal for His Word and a love for people. God has given Stetson such a love for people, he loves to talk to people and spend time with them. He desires to tell people about Jesus and his healing powers. He daily goes out into the world, filled with the Holy Spirit, and finds people to tell his story to, and how much God loves them. He has told his testimony at many churches, and this story has touched many lives. "All praise to God, the Father of our Lord Jesus Christ. God is our merciful Father and the source of all comfort. He comforts us in all of our troubles so that we can comfort others. When they are troubled, we will be able to give them the same comfort God has given us." 2 Corinthians 1:3-4. Stetson speaks of the great things that God gave us through our troubles so that he can comfort others through their troubles. I used to walk around filled with shame, not wanting people to know who I was for fear that they knew what Stetson was doing. Now, when people find out that I am his wife, they cannot tell me enough good things about him. I no longer fear someone talking to me about Stetson, because I know that God's grace has covered him. People are constantly telling me how funny he is, how kind he is, and how gracious he is. However, I know that it is not Stetson, but the Holy Spirit living through him. It is

God's love, kindness, and grace overflowing through him and pouring out onto others. Where Satan once had him filled with hate, anger, paranoia, and mistrust, God has filled him to overflowing with love, grace, kindness, mercy, and trust. God has touched so many people through Stetson and God's story of triumph in his life. God's story that he is telling through us is glorifying Him.

Stetson and I laugh about the things we did in the past because we cannot believe we acted that way. We just recently were laughing about the time I chased him out the front door begging him not to leave. I was trying to grab his pickup keys to keep him from driving while he was trying to stab me in the hand with them. Those chaotic things we did are so far behind us and so far away from the love we feel now that we have to laugh. We cannot believe we used to be the crazy people we were because God has brought us to such a peaceful and loving place. God has changed us so miraculously that our past seems like a distant memory that happened to different people. Looking at the Stetson I see and know now, I cannot imagine him acting like he did in the past. God made us new. "This means that anyone who belongs to Christ has become a new person. The old life is gone; a new life has begun!" 2 Corinthians 5:17. This is exactly what Christ has done in our lives. We are new creations. We can either cry and be somber about our sad and shameful past, or grab onto God's blessings we have today and laugh about the past. We choose to laugh. We choose to be thankful about the darkness and sin that God has delivered us from because His light shone through that darkness.

I still struggle with shame and isolation at times, but God has shown me a way through them. He has shown me that I do not have to allow Satan to shame me or isolate me. At times, I feel grief for the absence of happiness I had during my pregnancies. Satan tries to whisper envy into my heart when I see people enjoying their pregnancies and experiencing joy while pregnant. He tells me that I should feel robbed of the joy that I could have felt while being pregnant with my children. But I know that those feelings are traps. I see the joy and happiness that God has given me through my children, and I thank God that I was able to have them. I could dwell on all the negative and be bitter, or look to God and his kindness and love that He has for me now, and the love He had for me then. God gave us the power to triumph over Satan, his plans, and his deceit through Jesus Christ. Jesus tells us in Luke 10:19, "Look, I have given you authority over all the power of the enemy, and you can walk among snakes and scorpions and crush them. Nothing will injure you." We live in a fallen world, so we will struggle with our flesh and with Satan's temptations, but we do not have to let them overwhelm us. Jesus Christ has given us authority to prevail! Satan and his ploys are below us because the One who is victorious lives within us! I do not have to feel shame for my past when Satan tries to trip me up and question myself. I do not have to feel isolated when Satan makes me feel alone. I am never alone. God Almighty is always with me. God commands us in Joshua 1:9, "This is my command-be strong and courageous! Do not be afraid or discouraged. For the Lord your God is with you wherever you go." He commands us to be strong and to triumph over Satan because we are not alone. I may let the world speak fear and condemnation to me at times, but I will not be overcome for God is with me.

"The thief's purpose is to steal and kill and destroy. My purpose is to give them a rich and satisfying life." John 10:10. Satan tried to destroy me. Satan tried to destroy Stetson. But God's purpose prevails. God saved us and redeemed us. God never left us alone. All the dark times we experienced, every awful fight, every awful day of pain and anguish, God was still there. He was there every moment, helping me through my pain, helping me survive each day, helping me take care of my daughter, and giving me the strength to carry on when my earthly mind was failing me. I could not have survived that life on my own. God was protecting me at every step. He was protecting Stetson and our children at every step. *God was there in every moment.* He was there because He loves us and He had a purpose for our lives. He has a purpose to give each one of us a rich, bountiful, and satisfying life. My family is redeemed and victorious because God loves us. Because of God, I do not have an island anymore. I have a firm foundation.

> For God saved us and called us to live a holy
> life. He did this, not because we deserved it,
> but because that was his plan from before
> the beginning of time-to show us his grace
> through Christ Jesus.
>
> -2 Timothy 1:9

CPSIA information can be obtained
at www.ICGtesting.com
Printed in the USA
BVHW072103130820
586223BV00004B/256